QUICK MEETING OPENERS FOR BUSY MANAGERS

QUICK
MEETING
OPENERS
FOR
BUSY MANAGERS

More Than 50 Icebreakers, Energizers,
and Other Creative Activities That Get Results

BRIAN COLE MILLER

⁴AMACOM

AMERICAN MANAGEMENT ASSOCIATION
New York | Atlanta | Brussels | Chicago | Mexico City | San Francisco
Shanghai | Tokyo | Toronto | Washington, D. C.

This publication is designed to provide accurate and authoritative information in regard to the subject matter covered. It is sold with the understanding that the publisher is not engaged in rendering legal, accounting, or other professional service. If legal advice or other expert assistance is required, the services of a competent professional person should be sought.

Library of Congress Cataloging-in-Publication Data

Miller, Brian Cole, 1956–

    Quick meeting openers for busy managers : more than 50 icebreakers,
energizers, and other creative activities that get results / Brian Cole Miller.

      p. cm.

    Includes index.

    ISBN 978-0-8144-0933-6

    1. Business meetings.   I. Title.

    HF5734.5.M55 2008

    658.4′56—dc22

                                        2008001117

Printing number

10 9 8 7 6 5 4 3 2 1

CONTENTS

ACKNOWLEDGMENTS

Once again, I owe a lot of gratitude to my friends and colleagues who shared their thoughts and ideas for this volume. Thank you.

Suzanne Famolare—You have so many great ideas, I wonder if you should write a book yourself!

Franca Little—I hope we get to do some of these fun activities together soon (in Sydney? London? Rio? Cape Town?)!

Carol Naylor—No one believes you when you say you're not good at this stuff. (Seriously, Carol, no one!)

Rick Ritacco—I'm sorry, but I could only include your G-rated ideas.

Kiki Dreyer Burke—I miss working with you, Kik-ster!

Chris Lowe—I know that you only contribute so you can see your name in print, so here it is again: CHRIS LOWE.

Sara Bonner—How do you find the time to help me on top of everything else you have going on?

Adam Bryant—See? You *did* learn something valuable at all those church youth group meetings.

Tony Lipscomb—Thanks for being my virtual sounding board on a lot of this stuff.

Steven Haines—You have to come to Ohio to get your free copy of this book, my friend!

Mark Hansen—I appreciate how freely you share stuff with me from sparkspace.

Wayne Miller—OK, I used your ideas, now will you let me contribute my ideas to your next textbook on biochemistry or exercise physiology?

My son Logan Miller—Who'd have thought all the money I'm dumping into your college education would start paying back by way of good ideas for my book?!

Thank you Christina Parisi and Adrienne Hickey at AMACOM. I appreciate your confidence in me, as well as your patience!

Thanks to my ever-supportive and loving family—Gail, Lynn, Roger, Theresa, Logan, Heidee, and Benjamin.

As always, thanks mostly to you, Tim. Where would I be—personally or professionally—without your love, support, and encouragement?

INTRODUCTION

Meeting openers are structured activities designed to help group members introduce themselves, energize (or relax!), and otherwise get ready to participate in a meeting. The openers are not usually connected to the topic of the meeting but rather serve as a vehicle for getting people to open up and feel comfortable with each other before getting to the actual meeting agenda. This is especially helpful when group members don't know each other very well, there are one or more cliques in the group, or the subject will be particularly demanding.

Some call these exercises *icebreakers*. The term refers to ships in the artic regions. These ships are designed to break the ice, allowing vessels behind them to pass more easily. In much the same way, meeting openers, or icebreakers, pave the way for people to interact and work together—easier and smoother. The icebreakers I've included are not just for the purpose of introducing team members to each other but also to break teams up into groups, get them energized, and brainstorm.

Meeting openers, or icebreakers, are different from team-building activities. Effective team-building activities have a customized, work-related learning objective. Meeting openers, on the other hand, always have the same, simple objective: to help people warm up for an upcoming meeting, whatever the meeting is. Basic introductions are sometimes a part of that warming up. (If you do need team-building activities, see my other two collections, *Quick Team-Building Activities for Busy Managers* and *More Quick Team-Building Activities for Busy Managers*.)

I've organized the meeting openers into six chapters. The first chapter has two *very* quick and easy meeting openers with dozens of variations. Use these when you are reviewing this book on your way to the meeting and don't have time to prep for anything else!

Many openers require that you break the group into smaller groups. Chapter 2 has almost 100 ideas for breaking groups in half, into pairs, and into other smaller teams.

Chapter 3 has icebreakers for introductions. Of course, the activities in the rest of the book may also be used for introductions, so don't dismiss them if you need an introduction activity. It's just that the ones in Chapter 3 are specifically designed for this purpose.

The rest of the openers are in Chapters 4, 5, and 6. They are organized by group sizes.

Chapter 4 has activities geared for smaller groups when you have enough time for all participants to speak, share, or introduce themselves to the whole group. Small groups don't have more than about 20 participants.

Groups that have 12 to 35 participants are the focus of Chapter 5. Here, the meeting openers may keep the participants together for limited full-group interaction or divide them up to allow for more interaction within the smaller groups.

Chapter 6 has activities that are good for groups of over 35 participants. The group is either broken into smaller, more manageable groups, or the participants mingle. If they mingle, there is structure, and there are specific objectives that will encourage (or even force) them to interact.

The outline for each meeting opener is easy to follow. Each one is presented in the same easy-to-read, bulleted format:

This is . . . explains briefly what the activity is.

Use it to . . . tells what the purpose of the exercise is.

Best group size . . . indicates the ideal group size.

Materials you'll need . . . tells you everything you will need for the activity. Most of the time it's nothing!

Here's how . . . outlines, step by step, how to conduct the activity.

For example . . . illustrates how the activity may play out, so you get a good sense of what to expect.

Tips for success . . . includes things that will help you run your exercise more effectively.

Try these variations . . . offers variations on the activity that can be used to spice it up, slow it down, or otherwise alter it for a slightly different experience. I also indicate here how to adjust the activity for other sized groups than the "ideal."

Relax, you won't find any of these types of activities here:

NO "touchy-feely" icebreakers in which participants have to touch each other a lot or share intimate thoughts and feelings (activities that push the manager into the role of psychologist rather than activity leader).

NO outdoor activities requiring large areas, nice weather, and physically fit participants.

NO handouts to prepare, copy, or distribute.

NO lengthy activities in which more time is spent warming up than on the real work to be done in the meeting. All activities last *less than 15 minutes.*

NO role-plays in which participants are given a fictitious role to act out or pretend.

Meeting openers are fun! Use them at the start of your next meeting and enjoy the benefits of a group that's more engaged and involved and, ultimately, more productive.

CHAPTER 1

 # Activities That Are Super Quick and Easy

All the activities in this book are quick and easy. But sometimes you don't have even 5 minutes to prepare for an activity. In these cases, use one of the following two meeting openers or one of the dozens of variations listed. Both of these activities are the quickest and easiest to facilitate ever!

What these two activities lack in terms of a "wow" factor, they make up for with maximum flexibility for use with any group size, group configuration, time frame, materials required (none), and prep time (a few seconds).

IF I WERE A _____

This is . . .	➤ An activity in which participants imagine they are someone or something else and discuss it.
Use it to . . .	➤ Warm up the group before a meeting.
Best group size . . .	➤ Unlimited.
Materials you'll need . . .	➤ No materials are necessary for this activity.

Here's how . . .	1. Participants finish the statement, "If I were an animal, I would be a _____ ."
	2. Participants form pairs, small teams, or one large circle, or they mingle about to discuss their answers.

For example . . .	➤ "If I were an animal, I would be a cheetah. Cheetah's are fast and seem to always be focused on their objective—just like me."
	➤ "If I were an animal, I would be an eagle. I've always wished I could fly!"

Tips for success . . .	➤ Don't give too many examples; let the participants be creative.
	➤ Don't be too strict on the rules. For example, if someone says he or she would be a bee, allow it, even though a bee is an insect, not an animal.

Try these
variations . . .

If I Were a _____

- Fruit
- Cartoon character
- Automobile
- Food
- TV/movie character
- Superhero
- Piece of jewelry
- Key on a computer keyboard
- Color
- Toy
- Machine
- Piece of sports equipment
- Beverage
- Monster
- Musical instrument
- Toiletry or grooming accessory
- Piece of clothing
- Dessert
- Magazine
- Item in a mail order catalog
- Foreign country
- Plant
- Appliance
- Piece of furniture
- Item of footwear

QUESTIONS

This is . . .	➤ An activity in which participants respond to a thought-provoking question about themselves.
Use it to . . .	➤ Help a group warm up and start talking.
Best group size . . .	➤ Unlimited.
Materials you'll need . . .	➤ No materials are necessary for this activity.
Here's how . . .	1. Participants answer a question, such as, "What's your middle name, and why did your parents give it to you?" 2. Have participants form pairs, small teams, or one large circle or mingle about to discuss their answers.
For example . . .	➤ "My middle name is Kay. I have no idea where it came from. I think my parents just liked the way it went with my first name." ➤ "My middle name is John. My father wanted to honor some guy named John who had been like a father to him when he was growing up." ➤ "My parents never gave me a middle name. They assumed I'd get married, take my husband's name as my last name, and then use my last name as my middle name. So far this hasn't worked out for them!"

> "My middle name is Geneal. My mother wanted to name me after her favorite aunt, but my dad wouldn't let her, so they compromised and made her name my middle name."

Tips for success . . .
> Don't force people to go in order if you are seated in a circle. Some may need more time to think of a response or get the courage to share their response.

Try these variations . . .
> What kind of car do you drive and why?
> What is your favorite guilty pleasure?
> What would you like to be famous for?
> How do you like to celebrate your birthday?
> What's the biggest mistake you've ever made?
> Where would you live if you could live anywhere?
> What's one thing you would like to change about your physical appearance?
> If you could travel in time, when would that be?
> What did you want to be when you grew up?
> What song makes you start to dance every time you hear it?
> What's your best celebrity sighting?
> What is your biggest fear?
> What is one thing you want to be sure to do before you die?
> What habit do you wish you could break?
> Who would you love to have dinner with some evening (choose anyone living or dead)?
> If you were stranded on a deserted island and could have only one thing with you, what would it be?
> If you could have three wishes granted by a genie, what would they be?
> What was your first job?

- ➤ What one charity would you give a million dollars to if you could?
- ➤ What home improvement project would you love to have done?
- ➤ What song always gets stuck in your head once you hear it?

CHAPTER 2

Activities for Grouping People

Often activities work best when people are grouped together some-how—in pair, trios, or small groups—or when the whole group is split in half, into thirds, and so on. This chapter includes dozens of ways to do both.

The first section has techniques for getting participants into a specific size of team—pairs, trios, and foursomes, as well as any other size group you may want.

The second section has methods for getting a group split into a specific number of smaller groups, regardless of their size—two groups, three groups, four groups, as well as any other number of groups you may want from the whole.

When the activities in Chapters 3 through 6 call for the group to be divided up somehow, use these ideas for a seamless experience.

Grouping People by the Size of Team Regardless of the Number of Teams

Use these ideas and instructions for getting the group into pairs:

1. Turn to the person immediately to your left (or right, or behind you, or in front of you).
2. Find one other person with shoes similar to yours.
3. Find someone who lives in a different zip code than you.
4. Find one other person who is the same height as you.

5. Line up tallest to shortest and pair the tallest with the shortest, then the second tallest with the second shortest, and so forth.

6. Find one other person whose first (or last) name starts with the same letter as yours.

7. Find one other person whose birthday is in the same month as yours.

8. Find someone whose alma mater's colors (or at least one) are the same as yours.

9. Find one other person with the same horoscope sign as you.

10. Hand out dominos randomly to all participants, and ask them to find the person who has a matching domino.

11. Hand out playing cards randomly to all participants, and ask them to find the person who has a matching playing card.

12. Cut pictures from a magazine in half. Hand out the half pictures randomly to all participants, and ask them to find the person with the other half of their picture.

13. Have participants mingle until a prearranged signal is given. Then they pair up with the first person they can find, as quickly as possible.

14. Write corporate slogans on slips of paper. Write the names of the matching corporations on slips of paper. Hand all the slips of paper out randomly, and ask participants to find the person with the slogan or corporation that matches theirs.

15. Write common pairs on two slips of paper (Bonnie and Clyde, salt and pepper, black and white, peanut butter and jelly, etc.). Hand out all the slips of paper randomly, and ask participants to find the person who has the same pair. Note: It's ok if you don't have a different pairing for each pair of people. There can be many "salts" looking for one of many "peppers."

16. Provide name tags made of several different shapes, and ask participants to find someone who has a matching shape.

17. Everyone rolls a die. Those who throw an even number will pair up with someone who throws an odd number.

Use these ideas and instructions for getting the group into trios:

1. Turn to the person immediately to your left and right.
2. Find two people with shoes similar to yours.
3. Find two people who are the same height as you.
4. Find two people who live in different zip codes than you.
5. Find two people whose first (or last) name starts with the same letter as yours.
6. Find two people whose birthdays are in the same month as yours.
7. Find two people whose alma mater's colors (or at least one) are the same as yours.
8. Find two people with the same horoscope sign as you.
9. Hand out dominos randomly to all participants, and ask them to find two people with a matching domino.
10. Hand out playing cards randomly to all participants, and ask them to find two people with a matching playing card.
11. Cut cartoon strips into frames (most cartoons have three). Hand out a frame randomly to all participants, and ask them to find people with frames that complete their cartoon strip.
12. Have participants mingle until a prearranged signal is given. Then they get into a trio with the first two people they can find, as quickly as possible.
13. Write common trios on two slips of paper (Snap, Crackle, and Pop; do, re, and mi; Moe, Larry, and Curly; Big Mac, fries, and Coke, etc.). Hand out all the slips of paper randomly, and ask participants to find two people to complete their set. Note: It's ok if you don't have a different pairing for each pair of people. There can be many "Snaps" looking for one of many "Crackles," and together they will seek one of many "Pops."
14. Write the lyrics of a popular song on three slips of paper (one line per slip). Make enough duplicate slips of paper for everyone. Randomly hand out the slips of paper, and ask participants to find two other people to complete their song lyrics.

Alternatively, instead of duplicating the song, use a different song for each set of three slips of paper for every three participants.

15. Provide name tags made of several different shapes, and ask participants to find two people who have the same shape as theirs.

Use these ideas and instructions for getting the group into teams of four:

1. Use any of the activities above that will put people into pairs. Then use it again (or another one) with the pairs so that the pairs pair up.
2. Hand out playing cards randomly to all participants, and ask participants to team up with those who have the other three suits. (The face value of the card is irrelevant.)
3. Write four ingredients for tacos (tortilla, meat, salsa, cheese) on slips of paper (one ingredient on each slip). Hand out all the slips of paper randomly, and ask participants to find three other people who have the other ingredients needed to make a taco.
4. Form a group of four whose alma mater's colors (or at least one) are the same.
5. Cut cartoon strips into frames (use those with four frames). Hand out a frame randomly to all participants, and ask them to find people with frames that complete their cartoon strip.
6. Find three other people born in the three other seasons as the one you were born in (spring, summer, autumn, winter).
7. Form a group of four people, none of whom has the same horoscope sign. Alternatively, form a group of four people who all share the same sign.
8. Find three other people who have the same number children as you do.
9. Have the group mingle until a prearranged signal is given. Then, participants are to team up as quickly as possible with the three people closest to them.

10. Write the lyrics of a popular song on four slips of paper (one line per slip). Make enough duplicate slips of paper for everyone. Randomly hand out the slips of paper, and ask participants to find three other people to complete their song lyrics. Alternatively, use a different song for each set of four slips of paper for every four participants.

11. Provide name tags made of several different shapes, and ask participants to find three others with matching shapes.

12. Write the names of four animals that can be acted out (the monkey scratching his armpits, the bull with horns, etc.) on slips of paper. Randomly hand out the slips of paper. Ask participants to act like their animals and then form groups of four animals with no duplicates in each group. No speaking or noises are allowed.

Use these ideas for getting the group into teams with X number of participants:

1. Write X ingredients for tacos (tortilla, meat, salsa, cheese, onions, etc.) on slips of paper (one ingredient on each slip). Hand out all the slips of paper randomly, and ask participants to find X people who have the other ingredients needed to make a taco.

2. Form a group of X whose alma mater's colors (or at least one) are the same.

3. Cut cartoon strips into frames (use those with X frames). Hand out a frame randomly to all participants, and ask them to find X people with frames that complete their cartoon strip.

4. Form a group of X people, none of whom has the same horoscope sign. Alternatively, form a group of X people who all share the same sign.

5. Form a group of X people, all of whom have the same number children.

6. Have the group mingle until a prearranged signal is given. Then they are to team up as quickly as possible to make a group of X.

7. Write the lyrics of a popular song on X slips of paper (one line per slip). Make enough duplicate slips for everyone. Randomly hand out the slips of paper, and ask participants to form groups of X people to complete the song lyrics. Alternatively, use a different song for each set of X slips of paper for every X participants.

8. Provide name tags made of several different shapes, and ask participants to form groups of X with matching shapes.

9. Write X drinks (margarita, martini, screwdriver, mojito, etc.) on slips of paper (one drink on each slip). Hand out all the slips of paper randomly and ask participants to form groups of X with no duplicate drinks.

10. Write the names of X animals that can be acted out (the monkey scratching his armpits, the bull with horns, etc.) on slips of paper. Randomly hand out the slips. Participants act like their animals and form groups of X based on the animal motions. No speaking or noises are allowed.

Grouping People by the Number of Teams Regardless of the Size of Each Team

Use these ideas and instructions for splitting the group into two teams:

1. Count off one, two, one, two, one, two, until everyone has been counted. All ones are one team; all two are the other.

2. With smaller groups, have all participants close their eyes. You walk among them, randomly tapping them on their shoulder. Tap every other one on the left shoulder. All those tapped on their left shoulder are one team; those tapped on their right shoulder are on the other team.

3. Have the group line up tallest to shortest, by birthday (month and day only), longest to shortest tenure with your organization, distance traveled to come to the meeting, and so forth. Find the middle of the line, and split the group in half there.

4. Have participants pair up with the person closest to them and each pair plays Paper, Scissors, Rock. Winners are on one team; losers are on the other.

5. Have participants pair up with the person closest to them and compare the lengths of their names (number of letters). Those with the longer name are on one team, and those with the shorter name are on the other.

6. Give everyone a playing card. Those with a red card are on one team, and those with a black card are on the other.

7. Split the group by birthdays. Participants with a birthday in January through June are one team, and those with birthdays in July through December are the other team. If the teams are uneven, adjust the dates (weeks or one month at a time) until the teams even out.

8. Split the group by first or last names. Participants with names that start with A through L are one team, and those with names that start with M through Z are the other team. If the teams are uneven, adjust the letters one at a time until the teams even out.

Use these ideas and instructions for splitting the group into three teams:

1. Count off one, two, three, one, two, three, one, two, three until everyone has been counted. All ones are one team, all twos are another team, and all threes are the last team.

2. Have the group line up tallest to shortest, by birthday (month and day only), longest to shortest tenure with your organization, distance traveled to come to the meeting, and so forth. Divide the line into thirds to create three teams.

3. Give everyone a playing card. Remove one whole suit first. Teams are based on the suits of the cards.

4. For smaller groups, have participants all close their eyes. You walk around the group and randomly tap them on their shoulders. Tap one, two, or three taps. All those tapped once are one

team, those tapped twice are another team, and those tapped three times are the last team.

5. Split the group by birthdays. January through April birthdays comprise one team, May through August birthdays comprise another team, and September through December birthdays comprise the third team. If the teams are uneven, adjust the dates (weeks or one month at a time) until the teams even out.

6. Split the groups by first or last names. Names that start with A through I comprise one team, names that start with J through Q comprise another team, and names that start with R through Z comprise the third team. If the teams are uneven, adjust the letters one at a time until the teams even out.

7. Write the names of three very common songs ("Row, Row, Row Your Boat," "Happy Birthday," "Twinkle, Twinkle Little Star," etc.) on slips of paper, and randomly hand them out. Participants hum their song and form groups based on a common tune.

8. Write the names of three animals that make sounds (dog, bird, cow, cat, pig, etc.) on slips of paper, and randomly hand them out. Participants make the sound of their animal and form groups based on the same animal sounds.

9. Write the names of three animals that can be acted out (the monkey scratching his armpits, the bull with horns, etc.) on slips of paper, and randomly hand them out. Participants make the motion of their animal and form groups based on the same motions. No speaking or noises are allowed.

10. Provide name tags made of three different shapes. Everyone with the same shape is on the same team.

Use these ideas and instructions for splitting the group into four teams:

1. Count off one, two, three, four, one, two, three, four, one, two, three, four until everyone has been counted. All ones are a team, all twos are a team, all threes are a team, and all fours are a team.

2. Have participants line up tallest to shortest, by birthday (month and day only), longest to shortest tenure with your

organization, distance traveled to the meeting, and so forth. Divide the line to create four teams.

3. Give everyone a playing card. Teams are based on the suits of the cards.

4. Split the group by birthdays. January through March birthdays comprise a team, April through June birthdays comprise a team, and so forth. If the teams are uneven, adjust the dates (a few weeks or one month at a time) until the teams even out.

5. Split the group according to first or last names. Names that start with A through G comprise one team, names that start with H through M comprise another team, and so forth. If the teams are uneven, adjust the letters one at a time until the teams even out.

6. Write the names of four very common songs ("Row, Row, Row Your Boat," "Happy Birthday," "Twinkle, Twinkle Little Star," etc.) on slips of paper, and randomly hand them out. Participants hum their song and form groups based on a common tune.

7. Write the names of four animals that make sounds (dog, bird, cow, cat, pig, etc.) on slips of paper, and randomly hand them out. Participants make the sound of their animal and form groups based on the same animal sounds.

8. Write the names of four animals that can be acted out (the monkey scratching his armpits, the bull with horns, etc.) on slips of paper, and randomly hand them out. Participants make the motion of their animal and form groups based on the same motions. No speaking or noises are allowed.

9. Provide name tags made of four different shapes. Everyone with the same shape is on the same team.

10. Write four ingredients for tacos (tortilla, meat, salsa, cheese) on slips of paper (one ingredient on each slip). Hand out all the slips of paper randomly. Everyone with the same ingredient is on the same team.

11. Ask participants to go into one of the four corners of the room based on their birth order: oldest, youngest, middle (anyone not oldest or youngest), and only child.

Use these ideas for splitting the group into X number of teams:

1. Count off one, two, three . . . X, one, two, three . . . X, and so forth. All ones are on a team, all twos are on a team, all threes are on a team . . . all Xs are on a team, and so forth.

2. Have participants line up tallest to shortest, by birthday (month and day only), longest to shortest tenure with your organization, distance traveled to come to the meeting, and so forth. Divide the line to create X teams.

3. Split the group by first or last names. Divide the alphabet into X groupings. Names that start with the first grouping are one team, names that start with the second grouping are another team, and so on. If the teams are uneven, adjust the letters one at a time until they even out.

4. Prepare deck(s) of playing cards in advance. Use a different value card for each team that will be created. Randomly give everyone a playing card. All those with the same value card are on the same team.

5. Write X ingredients for tacos (tortilla, meat, salsa, cheese, onions, etc.) on slips of paper (one ingredient on each slip), and randomly hand them out. Everyone with the same ingredient is on the same team.

6. Mark ping pong balls with numbers 1 through X. Make one for each person in the group. Have participants each pick a ball and form a team with all the others who have matching numbers.

7. Write the names of X very common songs ("Row, Row, Row Your Boat," "Happy Birthday," "Twinkle, Twinkle Little Star," etc.) on slips of paper, and randomly hand them out. Participants hum their song and form groups based on the same song.

8. Write the names of X animals that make sounds (dog, bird, cow, cat, pig, etc.) on slips of paper, and randomly hand them out. Participants make the sound of their animal and form groups based on the same sounds.

9. Write the names of X animals that can be acted out (the monkey scratching his armpits, the bull with horns, etc.) on slips of paper, and randomly hand them out. Participants make the motion of their animal and form groups based on the same motions. No speaking or noises are allowed.
10. Provide name tags made of X different shapes. Everyone with the same shape is on the same team.
11. Write X drinks (margarita, martini, screwdriver, mojito, etc.) on slips of paper (one drink on each slip). Hand out all the slips of paper randomly. Everyone with the same drink is on the same team.

CHAPTER 3

Icebreakers for Introductions

Although most meeting starters *can* be used to help people introduce themselves, the activities in this section are particularly aimed at doing just this. And yes, although any of them *could* be used with people who already know each other, you'll find them more effective with people who don't. They also work well with two separate groups that are coming together for the first time, when the members of each group know their own group but not the other one—like during a merger of two departments.

All the icebreakers in this section can work for any size group. Some are better suited for larger groups, some for smaller. Regardless of what ideal group size is listed for the activity, I've included tips for adjusting for larger or smaller groups when applicable.

The key to successful introductions in larger groups is to not plan for everyone to meet everyone else. It's usually not practical, and sometimes it's not even possible. Besides, the human brain can learn only so many new names at once! So set your sights on helping everyone meet a few new people, people with whom they can network for the day. If there are future meetings, the realm of people they know will grow each time and at a pace that they can handle.

BLANKET NAMES

This is . . . ➤ An icebreaker activity in which participants learn each other's names and then try to be the first to say each other's name when a blanket between them is dropped.

Use it to . . . ➤ Help participants remember each other's names.

Best group size . . . ➤ Unlimited but best with fewer than 30 participants.

Materials you'll need . . . ➤ One large sheet or blanket.

Here's how . . .
1. Divide the group in half.
2. One participant from each team holds the blanket up between the teams and is out of play for that round.
3. Each team then selects one player to stand behind the blanket opposite each other.
4. The blanket is dropped.
5. The first person on either side of the blanket to call out the other person's name wins that round.
6. The person whose name was called is recruited to the winning team.
7. Repeat steps 2 through 6 for several rounds or until one team is eliminated.

| **Tips for** | ➤ Use a large enough blanket that most of the team |
| success . . . | members can be hidden behind it. |

➤ Sheets can work better because they are not as heavy, but be careful that participants cannot easily see through them.

➤ Have teams rotate the role of "blanket holder" so that no one's arms get too tired and so that everyone gets a chance behind the blanket.

Try these   ➤ Rather than call out the person's name, have par-
variations . . .   ticipants call out the person's location, job title, or other piece of information that would be important for everyone to remember.

➤ This icebreaker can work for much larger groups by first dividing them into smaller teams. There must be one blanket for each two teams. Alternatively, line up two to three people at the blanket each time and have them call out the name of the person opposite them.

BOUNCING BALLS

This is . . . ➤ An icebreaker activity in which participants say each other's names as they bounce a ball to each other.

Use it to . . . ➤ Help participants learn each other's names.

Best group size . . . ➤ Up to about 40.

Materials you'll need . . . ➤ One large ball that bounces well on the floor of the meeting room.

Here's how . . .

1. Participants stand in a circle.
2. Everyone announces his or her name.
3. The first person takes the ball and bounces it once to another participant while saying that person's name. After bouncing the ball, participants fold their arms to indicate they have already had the ball (and not to throw it to them again).
4. The next participant catches the ball and immediately bounces it to someone else, saying that person's name (and then folding his or her arms).
5. If someone misses a name or the ball, start over, but the ball is bounced to someone different this time.
6. Repeat steps 3 through 5 above until the ball has made it to everyone in the group. Then play

another round, but instruct participants not to bounce it to the same person they did before.

Tips for success . . . ➤ The kind of ball used for Four Square is good for this game too.

Try these variations . . . ➤ Add a second ball simultaneously to the game (this will make it very confusing!).

➤ Make the game faster by using a soft handball and tossing it rather than bouncing it.

➤ After everyone has learned everyone's name, play the game again, this time announcing their job, location, or other relevant information that's important for everyone to know.

➤ Speed things up and by playing the game more like Four Square. Rather than catching the ball, merely tap it to bounce to the next person. This will make the game quicker and much more challenging.

➤ This activity can work for much larger groups by first dividing them into smaller teams. Be sure to have a ball for each group.

BUMPER CARS

This is . . .	➤ An icebreaker activity in which participants move around the space as if they are driving bumper cars and then collide with others for conversation.
Use it to . . .	➤ Help participants in large groups meet each other.
Best group size . . .	➤ Unlimited.
Materials you'll need . . .	➤ A whistle (or other noisemaker).
Here's how . . .	1. Have participants move around the space as if they are driving bumper cars.
	2. Blow the whistle in three short blasts.
	3. Everyone must now "collide" (as with bumper cars) with two other people to form an "accident" of three. Tell participants to be gentle.
	4. In the threesome, participants introduce themselves. They can give their names, some work-related information and perhaps what kind of car they drive.
	5. After 60 seconds, blow the whistle once, and everyone starts driving around again.
	6. Repeat steps 2 through 5 several times.

For example . . .	➤ "Hi, my name is Kenji. I've been with the firm 4 years and I work in Accounting. I drive a Honda Accord." "Hi, Kenji, my name is Chris. I've been here 14 years. I work in Sales and I drive a Beemer." "Hi guys, I'm Keiko. I started here right out of college and . . . oops, there goes the whistle!"
Tips for success . . .	➤ Encourage them to have fun with the collisions! ➤ Encourage them to drive into new areas of the room to meet new people. ➤ Keep the time limits for introductions tight so they can meet as many participants as possible.
Try these variations . . .	➤ Vary the number of whistle blasts. The number of whistle blasts indicates how many participants should collide to form a conversation team. Three blasts means a team of three, four blasts means a team of four, and so forth.

BUMPITY-BUMP

This is . . .	➤ An icebreaker activity in which participants have to say the names of those on either side of them quickly.
Use it to . . .	➤ Help participants learn each other's names.
Best group size . . .	➤ Up to about 40.
Materials you'll need . . .	➤ No materials are necessary for this activity.
Here's how . . .	1. Have the group sit in a circle. You stand in the middle.
	2. Give participants a moment to learn the names of the persons on both sides of them.
	3. Approach someone, say his or her name, and then say, "bumpity-bump-bump-bump."
	4. While you are saying "bumpity-bump-bump-bump," the person whose name you called must quickly say the names of the people on both sides of him or her.
	5. If you finish saying "bumpity-bump-bump-bump" before the person says the names, trade places and he or she is now in the center. Then repeat steps 3 and 4.
	6. If he or she beats you, you repeat step 3 and 4 with someone else in the group.

7. After someone is in the center more than three turns, he or she may say, "bumpity-bump-bump-bump" without a name. When this happens, everyone switches seats and play resumes (repeating steps 2 through 6).

Tips for success . . .

➤ Go slowly at first, giving participants a chance to build their confidence and see how the game is played before ripping off "bumpity-bump-bump-bump" more quickly.

➤ You may have to remind them that they can say "bumpity-bump-bump-bump" to mix the room up only after three turns. Usually it gets easier for the person in the middle right after that.

Try these variations . . .

➤ Give participants a bit longer to react by saying "bumpity-bumpity-bumpity-bump."

➤ Make it more difficult by requiring first and last names to be said.

➤ This activity can work for much larger groups by first dividing them into smaller teams.

CHAMPIONS

This is . . .	➤ An icebreaker activity in which participants introduce each other so that others see what strengths they have.
Use it to . . .	➤ Introduce participants to each other in a positive, upbeat way that emphasizes each participant's value to the group.
Best group size . . .	➤ Up to about 20.
Materials you'll need . . .	➤ No materials are necessary for this activity.
Here's how . . .	1. Have participants pair up.
	2. Allow 5 minutes for participants to interview each other and learn more about each other.
	3. Each participant then introduces his or her partner to the group.
	4. The introduction should "sell" the person on how great he or she is and on how he or she will significantly contribute to the meeting or the task at hand.
For example . . .	➤ "This is Heidee. She's been with the company for only a short time. She brings a different perspective, yes. But more importantly, she's very good at helping people work together. She helps find

bridges and commonalities among differing opinions, and she can do this without making anyone feel like they 'won' or 'lost.' "

Tips for success . . .

➤ Make sure participants understand that the goal is not just to introduce their partner. The goal is to champion them, to show the rest of the group what a great asset their partner is to the meeting, team, or work group.

Try these variations . . .

➤ Have participants work in teams of three. Two people introduce and champion the third one.

➤ If time is limited, or if you want to reinforce self-confidence, don't have participants pair up. Rather, each participant introduces himself or herself. During their introduction, participants champion themselves, explaining what value they bring to the group.

➤ This activity can work for much larger groups by first dividing them into smaller teams.

DO YOU KNOW ME?

This is . . .   ➤ An icebreaker activity in which participants ask questions of each other about one other person in the group.

Use it to . . .   ➤ Help large groups mingle a bit and better get to know at least one other person in the group.

Best group size . . .   ➤ Up to about 40.

Materials you'll need . . .   ➤ Index cards with a different participant's name on each one.

Here's how . . .

1. Distribute the cards to the participants, making sure no one gets his or her own name.
2. Have the group mingle while holding their cards out and asking, "Do you know me?"
3. When someone answers "yes," the participant will ask a few questions about the name he or she has and can jot down notes on the card.
4. Then the two move on and gather more information.
5. After several minutes, have participants find the person whose name they have and introduce themselves briefly.

For example . . .	➤ "Do you know me?"
	➤ "Yes."
	➤ "Great, so which region do I work in?"
	➤ "Region 4."
	➤ "Okay, and how long have I worked for this company?"
	➤ "Oh, I'd say about 5 years, I think."
Tips for success . . .	➤ This activity works best with large groups in which everyone knows only a few participants well.
Try these variations . . .	➤ For smaller groups: after step 4, have each participant introduce the person whose name they researched.
	➤ This activity also works well when two groups that know themselves but not each other are coming together. In this case, make sure they all get each other's names.

 **HANDSHAKES**

This is . . .	➤ An icebreaker activity in which participants mingle and shake hands with each other several different ways.
Use it to . . .	➤ Loosen the group up, meet several other participants, and get physically active.
Best group size . . .	➤ Unlimited.
Materials you'll need . . .	➤ No materials are necessary for this activity.
Here's how . . .	1. All participants mingle with each other.
	2. Participants shake hands with the first three people they meet and then introduce themselves.
	3. Participants give a "high five" greeting to the next five people they meet and then introduce themselves.
	4. Participants "hit the rock" (butt fists together) with the next three people they meet and then introduce themselves.
	5. Participants create their own unique greeting (different from a handshake, high five, or fist butting) and use it with the next three people they meet and then introduce themselves.

For example . . .

> ➤ Amanda has met three people. Adam has met only two. When Adam and Amanda meet, Adam will shake hands with Amanda before introducing himself. Amanda will then give Adam a high five before she introduces herself.

Tips for success . . .

> ➤ Always follow the protocol. It may help to post the order for all to see.

Try these variations . . .

> ➤ Have participants go in order of the greetings for three rounds. Rather than greet the first three people with a handshake, greet the first with a handshake, the second with a high five, and so on. After all four greetings have been used, go back to the first one (the handshake) again, and so on.

LOGOS

This is . . .   ➤ An icebreaker activity in which participants put a logo on their name tag that they most identify with.

Use it to . . .   ➤ Help large groups start to learn each other's names and get to know each other better.

Best group size . . .   ➤ Unlimited.

Materials you'll need . . .   ➤ A name tag for each participant.
➤ A pen for each participant.

Here's how . . .   1. Have participants write their name on their name tag.
2. Next to their name, participants are to put a corporate logo that they identify with strongly.
3. Have the participants mingle, sharing with each other why they chose the logo they did.

For example . . .   ➤ "My name is Rosie, and this logo is the Nike swoosh. I chose it because I tend to be impulsive and 'just do it' when faced with a situation. I also like sports."
➤ "My name is Kiki, and this logo is from a bed and breakfast I stayed at in Portland, Maine. I identify with it because it just feels calm and even keeled,

which is what everyone says I am: calm and even keeled."

Tips for success . . .

➤ Allow the group to use logos that are famous or create their own. Beware that creating their own will take most participants much more time, though.

Try these variations . . .

➤ Rather than logos, have participants use a famous tag line or marketing slogan.

➤ Break the group into small teams of four to six members. Have the team choose a logo that best represents them. Alternatively, choose a logo that best represents the project or the whole work group they belong to.

MIND READER

This is . . .	➤ An icebreaker activity in which participants ask each other yes/no questions in an effort to guess what is on the other's mind.
Use it to . . .	➤ Help large groups start meeting each other.
Best group size . . .	➤ Unlimited.
Materials you'll need . . .	➤ No materials are necessary for this activity.
Here's how . . .	1. Participants mingle freely.
	2. Each participant tries to read someone else's mind by coming up with an idea and then testing it by asking yes/no questions.
	3. As long as the response is "yes," participants keep asking more questions. Once a response is "no," it is the other person's turn to ask questions.
	4. When a "no response" is given, both move on to other people.
For example . . .	➤ "Do you love chocolate?"
	➤ "Yes."
	➤ "I knew it! And do you eat chocolate at least every day?"
	➤ "Yes."
	➤ "And is your favorite chocolate dark chocolate?" "

- "No."
- "Hmm, okay, your turn."
- "Okay, do you wish you were somewhere else than here?"
- "Yes."
- "Do you wish you could be at the beach relaxing with a Margarita in one hand and a good book in the other?"
- "No."
- Both participants find a new partner to mind read.

Tips for success . . .
- Don't limit the topics. Half the fun is the way different people will ask about bizarrely different topics.
- Encourage them to not try too hard—it's supposed to be more fun than accurate!

Try these variations . . .
- Have the group form trios to ask the questions, two on one.
- Provide focus by giving the group a topic to learn about. For example, the goal could be to mind read others' favorite food, so the participants ask questions only about food.

 MY LETTER

This is . . .	➤ An icebreaker activity in which participants introduce themselves with words that all begin with the same letter—a letter they chose for themselves.
Use it to . . .	➤ Help groups get to know each other better than just their names.
Best group size . . .	➤ Up to about 20.
Materials you'll need . . .	➤ No materials are necessary for this activity.

Here's how . . .

1. Have everyone select a letter from the alphabet and announce it to the group or at least to a neighbor.
2. Give participants 2 minutes to think of as many words as they can to describe themselves. All words must begin with their chosen letter.
3. Have each participant share the words with the group.

For example . . .

➤ "My name is Amin, and my letter is K. The K words that describe me are kind, knuckleheaded, kisser, and king-like."

➤ "My name is Greta. My letter is P. My words are patient, practical, (o)pinionated, and pretty creative!"

Tips for success . . .

- ➤ When sharing the words, participants do not elaborate or embellish, just say the words.
- ➤ It's okay if several people choose the same letter.

Try these variations . . .

- ➤ Have participants write their words down and mingle with others, showing their words but not talking. They are encouraged to later follow up with people they found intriguing.
- ➤ Have participants post their words with their names on the walls for everyone to view throughout the day.
- ➤ This activity can work for much larger groups by first dividing the group into smaller teams.

PHYSICAL DESCRIPTIONS

This is . . .   ➤ An icebreaker activity in which participants write a physical description of themselves and then others try to match the descriptions with the right person.

Use it to . . .   ➤ Help the participants meet each other quickly.

Best group size . . .   ➤ Up to about 40.

Materials you'll need . . .
➤ An index card for each participant.
➤ A pen for each participant.

Here's how . . .
1. Give participants 3 minutes to write a physical description of themselves on their cards.
2. Shuffle the cards and redistribute them, one to each participant.
3. Participants read the description on their card, find the person who wrote it, and introduce themselves to that person.

For example . . .   ➤ "I'm average height for a man. I shave my head bald and have a goatee. I have blue eyes and a fair complexion."

> "I'm short, fat, and old! Actually, I just look old. I got this gray hair long before I should have. Also, I'm only a little fat. I need to lose about 25 pounds."

Tips for success . . .

> Encourage participants to write legibly so that others can easily read the description.
> Make sure no one gets his or her own card.
> Instruct participants not to include a description of the clothes they are wearing (this makes it too easy).
> Help participants who are having trouble finding the person described on the card.

Try these variations . . .

> For smaller groups, after step 2, participants try to guess who their card belongs to (without asking anyone) and write that person's name on the back. Then, participants swap cards and do the same with the next card. After several rounds, continue with step 3.
> This activity can work for much larger groups by first dividing them into smaller teams.

POLITE CATCH

This is . . . ➤ A ball game in which participants use each other's names as they toss and catch the ball.

Use it to . . . ➤ Help participants learn and remember each other's names.

Best group size . . . ➤ Up to aabout 40.

Materials you'll need . . . ➤ One soft ball.

Here's how . . .

1. Have participants stand in a circle.
2. Give the ball to one person.
3. This person tosses the ball to anyone in the circle.
4. Upon catching the ball, the participant is to thank the person who threw it to them using his or her name.
5. The thrower of the ball responds by saying "you're welcome" and using the catcher's name.
6. The thrower folds his or her arms to indicate he or she is out of the game now.
7. The catcher throws the ball to someone else.
8. Repeat steps 4 through 7 until everyone has had the ball once.
9. Then repeat the game again, requiring that participants throw the ball to someone else this round.

For example . . .	➤ "Thank you, Dean."
	➤ "You're welcome, Antonio."
	➤ "Thank you, Antonio."
	➤ "You're welcome, Rick."

Tips for success . . .	➤ Set a time limit (5 to 10 seconds) for someone to remember the other person's name before getting help from the group.
	➤ People who need help remembering someone's name shouldn't fold their arms and take themselves out of the game yet.

Try these variations . . .	➤ Speed things up. See how fast the group can go through a round.
	➤ Eliminate the arms folding part. Instead, have the game go quickly and see how many times the ball can be tossed around the group.
	➤ If someone can't remember a name, have everyone unfold their arms and play starts again for the whole group.
	➤ This activity can work for much larger groups by first dividing them into smaller teams. Make sure you have a ball for each team.

RIP IT UP

This is . . . ➤ An icebreaker activity in which participants make personal name tags by tearing a shape from a piece of construction paper.

Use it to . . . ➤ Give large groups conversation starters as they wait for the meeting to begin.

Best group size . . . ➤ Unlimited.

Materials you'll need . . .
➤ One piece of construction paper per person.
➤ A straight pin, tape, or some other method for attaching the name tag to each participant.
➤ Plenty of markers.

Here's how . . .
1. Give each participant a piece of paper, a marker, and a pin.
2. Each participant tears his or her paper into a shape that is symbolic for him or her.
3. Each participant writes his or her name on the shape and pins it on.
4. Participants mingle with each other using the shapes as a conversation starter.

For example . . . ➤ "Hi. My name is Jamal. This shape is supposed to be the happy and sad facemasks that represent drama. I love to be on stage and entertain as an actor. I only wish I could do it more often!"

➤ "Hello. I'm Rachel. No, this isn't a boot; it's a map of Italy. It's my favorite place on earth. I've lived there twice and always welcome a chance to go back. Oh, and yes, I speak fluent Italian, too!"

Tips for success . . .

➤ Use only dark-colored markers (avoid red, yellow, orange, pink, etc.) so that the names are easy to read from a foot or two away.

➤ You don't need one marker for every participant, but have plenty available so that waiting for the marker doesn't delay the activity unnecessarily.

➤ Have plenty of colors of construction paper available. You don't want the last participants arriving to be "stuck" with a color they don't like or even resent having to use.

➤ The mingling should be fast. Encourage participants to spend no more than 60 seconds with each other before moving on.

Try these variations . . .

➤ Rather than mingle, have the group sit in a circle. Taking turns, each participant introduces himself or herself by explaining their shape briefly to the rest of the group.

➤ Later in the day, have the participants turn their tags around (so the shape still shows but the name is hidden). Who can remember the most names? How did the shapes help?

➤ Structure the mingling by having everyone pair up. Give the pairs 30 seconds to introduce themselves using their shapes. Blow a whistle to indicate it's time to switch partners.

➤ Encourage participants to keep their name tags on all day. They can mingle at breaks and during lunch.

SHARK!

This is . . .
➤ An icebreaker activity in which participants mingle and introduce themselves in smaller groups to avoid falling victim to a shark.

Use it to . . .
➤ Help large groups mingle and network.

Best group size . . .
➤ Unlimited.

Materials you'll need . . .
➤ No materials are necessary for this activity.

Here's how . . .
1. Have the participants start walking around. They are not to talk to anyone at this point, just keep "swimming."
2. Give a signal. Participants must then find two others to team up with to avoid being eaten by the shark.
3. Whoever doesn't have a trio to join falls victim to the shark. After briefly introducing himself or herself to the whole group, he or she fakes a horrible death and is out of play.
4. Then all trios spend exactly 1 minute introducing themselves to each other.
5. Give the signal again, and all trios break up and start "swimming" again.

6. On the third signal, participants must find only one other participant to pair up with to avoid falling victim to the shark.
7. Repeat steps 3 through 6.

Tips for success . . .

➤ You may want a whistle, bell, or other noisemaker to signal when the shark is spotted and when swimming is to begin.
➤ For each round either keep changing the number of participants that must group together to avoid the shark or limit the time (10 seconds) they have to do it. Otherwise, the group evens out and the shark takes no one down.

Try these variations . . .

➤ For smaller groups, play the activity until there is only one survivor.
➤ Have the victims of the shark become sharks after they are killed off. At step 2, the shark(s) swarm and latch onto their victims before than can form a trio of safety.

SPEAKING IN TONGUES

This is . . .	➤ An icebreaker activity in which participants introduce themselves in a made up language, interpreted by their partner.
Use it to . . .	➤ Help groups warm up together and have a laugh.
Best group size . . .	➤ Up to about 20.
Materials you'll need . . .	➤ No materials are necessary for this activity.

Here's how . . .

1. Have participants pair up.
2. Each participant introduces himself or herself by speaking only in a made up language.
3. As the participant speaks in this language, his or her partner will act as interpreter and translate for the group.
4. The interpreter is guessing at what is being said (based on facial expressions, length of statements, gestures, etc.), because the language is truly being made up on the spot.
5. Participants should not discuss this ahead of time. The interpreter will be winging it, based solely on length of statements made, facial expressions, gestures, and so forth.

For example . . .	➤ "Sdjk fn wnf fnewqN."
	➤ "Gail."
	➤ "Jfewiqf fniewq."
	➤ "Yes, my partner says her name is fnewqN, but in English that's Gail."
	➤ "Wivmnw aqv qffewi vnoz qpfw qfo dsox losgss."
	➤ "She says she's been a teacher for 3 years."
	➤ "HH!! Wfokf!!" (with hand signals).
	➤ "Oh, sorry, she says that's 30 years, not 3."
	➤ "Xove sof iwppw ww apoxos cpps f ff ao."
	➤ "She says she loves teaching even more than chocolate chip cookies."
Tips for success . . .	➤ The made up language does not have to be consistent or logical. Just spewing gobbledygook is usually best (and funniest!).
	➤ Giving a format for the introductions may help participants feel more confident—name, number of years at the organization, and so forth.
	➤ Participants should not use a real foreign language.
	➤ Limit the introduction time to 1 minute per participant.
	➤ Reassure the interpreters that this is for fun and laughs. No one expects anyone to get things right!
Try these variations . . .	➤ Pair up people who know each other well, and see how close the translation is to the original message.
	➤ In truly bilingual groups, have participants introduce themselves in one language and their interpreter translate into the other.
	➤ Don't give participants time to correct the translation until later in the meeting, perhaps spreading it out throughout the entire meeting.
	➤ This activity can work for much larger groups by first dividing them into smaller teams.

SPEECHLESS

This is . . . ➤ An icebreaker activity in which participants introduce themselves to each other without speaking.

Use it to . . . ➤ Help groups learn more about each other and get physically active.

Best group size . . . ➤ Unlimited.

Materials you'll need . . . ➤ No materials are necessary for this activity.

Here's how . . .
1. Have participants pair up.
2. Give one person of the pair 60 seconds to communicate as much as possible about himself or herself without speaking.
3. Give a signal, and then the other person has 60 seconds to do the same.
4. Give a signal, and have everyone find a new partner.
5. Repeat steps 2 through 4.

Tips for success . . . ➤ Declare up front if drawing or writing is allowed.
➤ The person "listening" may speak to seek clarification or encourage his or her partner to provide more information.

**Try these
variations . . .**

➤ Do only one round. Afterward, have the pairs introduce each other to the rest of the group by speaking. The one being introduced may correct any misunderstandings presented by his or her partner.

➤ Rather than pairs, have participants form trios. The two listening can help each other understand the nonverbal one.

SURVIVOR

This is . . .	➤ An icebreaker activity in which participants mingle with a team and then vote two members off of the team.
Use it to . . .	➤ Warm up the group and have some fun.
Best group size . . .	➤ Unlimited.
Materials you'll need . . .	➤ No materials are necessary for this activity.
Here's how . . .	1. Have the group divide into teams of five to seven members.
	2. Allow 5 minutes for team members to introduce themselves and get to know each other a little bit.
	3. Tell the teams they must now vote two people off of their team by choosing the two who "fit in with the group a little bit too well" (leave this ambiguous!).
	4. Those voted off now go join other teams. Each team can take only two new members in, and they can't both be from the same prior team.
	5. Give the teams 5 more minutes to get acquainted with their new members.

Tips for
success . . .
   ➤ Don't give any more information about how the teams are to vote people off. Let them create their own criteria.

Try these
variations . . .
   ➤ Have teams vote people off who would make the best leader or the best communicator or some other complimentary attribute.

   ➤ Play another round. This time the team members who were voted off during the first round are immune to the next voting. Alternatively, they are the only ones who vote this time.

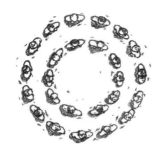

TWO CIRCLES

This is . . .
➤ An icebreaker activity in which participants form two circles and introduce themselves to each other in the circles.

Use it to . . .
➤ Help people meet and get to know each other quickly.

Best group size . . .
➤ Unlimited.

Materials you'll need . . .
➤ No materials are necessary for this activity.

Here's how . . .
1. Divide the group in half.
2. Form two circles, one inside the other.
3. The participants in the inside circle face the participants in the outside circle.
4. All participants have 30 seconds to introduce themselves to the person opposite them in the other circle.
5. After 30 seconds, everyone takes a large step to the right, faces another person in the other circle, and again introduces himself or herself to the person opposite.

Tips for success . . .
➤ It helps to give participants one or two topics to discuss as they introduce themselves (favorite animal, number of years in their field, birthplace, etc.).

Try these
variations . . .

➤ Rather than taking one step to the right, have the circles walk in opposite directions until you give the signal to stop, meet, and greet.

➤ After several rounds, have participants turn to the people on either side of them within their own circle to introduce themselves.

CHAPTER 4

Activities Best for Small Groups (Under 20)

Almost all of the activities in Chapter 4 require participants to say something that the rest of the group will listen to. For this reason, these activities work well only with smaller groups, less than 20 members. If you have the time, you can make them work for larger groups, but be careful. People can easily tire of listening to too many people taking turns. For larger groups, either split them up for these activities or find a more suitable one in Chapter 5 or 6.

Although designed primarily for larger groups, most of the activities in Chapters 5 and 6 are quite appropriate for smaller groups. Don't limit yourself to this chapter if you're working with a smaller group.

ARTIST

This is . . . ➤ An activity in which participants draw a picture and their partner "interprets" it for them.

Use it to . . . ➤ Warm the group up and have fun being creative on two levels.

Best group size . . . ➤ Up to about 20.

Materials you'll need . . . ➤ Paper and markers for each participant.

Here's how . . .
1. Independently, participants draw a picture that tells something about themselves.
2. Have participants put their name on their picture and pass them all to you.
3. Shuffle the pictures and distribute them randomly back to the group.
4. Participants take turns introducing the person whose picture they got.
5. The person doing the introduction will stand up, ask the person to be introduced to stand up, and then make the introduction by interpreting the picture.

For example . . . ➤ "This is Darryl. Let's see, this picture of a pen means that he likes to write and doodle a lot. Um, whenever he's in a meeting that gets boring, I think he takes out his pen and doodles away the time. Now this football next to the pen says he likes to play football, I think, or maybe he just likes to write about football?"

Tips for success . . .
> Discourage participants from chatting while drawing. If they do talk, restrict them from discussing the pictures they are drawing.
> Do not let participants include words in the drawings.
> You may or may not allow the person being introduced to correct any errors in the introduction. (If corrections are not given at this time, allow time durnig the break for people to mingle and provide clarification.)

Try these variations . . .
> Have the group break into pairs. Pairs interview each other for 5 minutes and then draw a picture about their partner. Participants then introduce their partner using the picture they drew or asking the partner to interpret the picture drawn of them.
> Divide larger groups into smaller teams of 6 to 12 members to use this activity.

DRESS FOR SUCCESS

This is . . . ➤ An activity in which participants share something about themselves based on one thing that they are wearing.

Use it to . . . ➤ Help groups warm up by talking about something they may not have given much thought to or something that has great meaning to them.

Best group size . . . ➤ Up to about 20.

Materials you'll need . . . ➤ No materials are necessary for this activity.

Here's how . . .
1. Participants sit in a circle.
2. Participants take turns telling a short story about something they are currently wearing—why they chose it to wear, or where they got it, and so forth.

For example . . . ➤ "I'm wearing these cool earrings that I got from my mother before she died. My dad says that apparently she wore them a lot and they're his favorites . . . and now they're my favorites, too!"

> "I got these pants when I was in Puerto Rico! I was there on business, and my luggage got lost so I had nothing to wear but what I had on. I went right out and picked these up. I'm surprised they're so comfortable up here, even in this weather."

Tips for success . . .
> Go first to show how much detail you want participants to go into.

Try these variations . . .
> This can be used as an icebreaker activity as well. Have them preface their story with a self-introduction.
> Limit the topic to jewelry only or to clothing only.
> Add an element of silliness by allowing participants to model their item. You may even create an area in the room to serve as the runway.
> Have participants select one thing they are wearing and tell what they would love to replace it with if they could.
> Divide larger groups into smaller groups of up to 12 members to use this activity.

FANTASY ISLAND

This is . . .
➤ An activity in which participants draw an island together on a large piece of paper.

Use it to . . .
➤ Help groups warm up and become better acquainted while being creative together.

Best group size . . .
➤ Up to about 20.

Materials you'll need . . .
➤ One large piece of flip chart or butcher paper.
➤ At least one marker per participant.

Here's how . . .
1. Seat everyone around the large piece of paper. The group is going to collectively draw an island on this piece of paper.
2. Participants begin by drawing part of the coastline near the edge of the paper in front of them. They can include any features they like.
3. Participants work together to join coastlines.
4. Participants then work inland, adding features to the island they feel are necessary.
5. Encourage everyone to work with their neighbors to coordinate or accommodate their inland features as well.

Tips for success . . .
➤ Have lots of colored markers for the group. Provide some with fine points and some with wide points for variation.

➤ Refrain from refereeing any disputes over the island construction. Let the group handle disagreements (and maybe discuss after the activity).

Try these variations . . .

➤ Give more structure to the island's purpose: a vacation spot for your group, an ideal island for your organization's relocation, and so forth.

➤ For larger groups, use an even larger piece of paper or divide the group into smaller teams. Have each team create an island. All the islands are part of an archipelago, and thus the teams will want to coordinate their efforts.

FORTUNE COOKIES

This is . . . ➤ An activity in which participants create fortunes for each other.

Use it to . . . ➤ Get a group energized and warmed up to each other before beginning the meeting.

Best group size . . . ➤ Up to about 20.

Materials you'll need . . .
➤ A pen for each participant.
➤ A 4″ × 4″ square piece of paper for each participant.

Here's how . . .
1. Distribute a pen and paper to every participant.
2. Each participant writes a fun fortune on his or her paper.
3. Participants fold the fortune up, and everyone swaps fortunes several times (the goal is to redistribute the fortunes so that no one knows who wrote the fortune he or she is holding).
4. Have fun reading the fortunes and discussing briefly.

For example . . .
➤ You will have one great idea during this meeting.
➤ Someone will forget your name today.
➤ Avoid the donuts this morning; pastries are okay though.
➤ The notes you take today will serve you well later on.

➤ You will meet someone with whom you will feel an instant connection.

Tips for success . . .

➤ Give several examples at the beginning rather than just a few. This will help participants broaden their interpretation of what a "good" fortune could include.

➤ Remind them to write legibly.

Try these variations . . .

➤ For groups that know each other somewhat, have participants write fortunes specifically for each other. Give each participant as many papers as there are other participants. Participants write a fortune for each other participant. Instruct participants not to include their names; the fortunes will be anonymous.

➤ After everyone has read his or her fortune, "recycle" the fortunes once or twice. Have participants fold the fortune back up and swap again several times. Participants read their second fortune and discuss briefly.

➤ Rather than fortunes, have the participants write challenges to each other. For example, "I challenge you to listen better than usual." "You are challenged to speak up when you would normally stay quiet." "I challenge you to help someone else participate better." After the meeting, ask participants about the success of meeting their challenges.

➤ Rather than giving fortunes to others, have participants predict something in their own future—perhaps just the future of the meeting ahead of them. At the end of the meeting, share the predictions and discuss the outcomes briefly.

➤ Divide larger groups into smaller teams of 8 to 20 members to use this activity.

FORTUNE TELLERS

This is . . .	➤ An activity in which participants anticipate or fantasize about their future.
Use it to . . .	➤ Warm the group up as well as get to know each other better.
Best group size . . .	➤ Up to about 20.
Materials you'll need . . .	➤ No materials are necessary for this activity.
Here's how . . .	1. Give participants 3 minutes to consider what they will be doing 5, 10, or 20 years from now. 2. Have each participant share his or her vision of the future with the rest of the group.
For example . . .	➤ "Five years from now, I suspect I'll be doing the same thing I am now. I'm not very ambitious. I love this kind of work. Of course, the way things are going here, I'm sure technology will have changed the way I do it!" ➤ "Twenty years from now I'll be retired and sipping margaritas on the beach brought to me by my own personal cabana boy!"

Tips for **success . . .**	➤ Allow the group to ask up to two questions of each speaker (especially if the speaker doesn't initially offer much insight into his or her thinking). For example, "Really? How do you think technology may change the way you do your job in the future?" ➤ Make sure the group doesn't judge or critique others. It's not about being right or wrong, it's about sharing vision and opening up about dreams.
Try these **variations . . .**	➤ Frame the scope of the future differently. For example, if a project has just been started, ask the group to anticipate the finished product or how much will be accomplished by a certain date. ➤ For groups that know each other well, have participants pair up and tell the fortune for their partner. ➤ Divide larger groups into smaller teams of 6 to 12 members to use this activity.

FUN FACTS

This is . . .	➤ An activity in which participants disclose something interesting about themselves and others try to guess who said what.
Use it to . . .	➤ Help the group get to know each other better and open dialogue.
Best group size . . .	➤ Up to about 20.
Materials you'll need . . .	➤ An index card for each participant. ➤ A pen for each participant.

Here's how . . .

1. Distribute an index card and a pen to each participant.
2. Give participants 3 minutes to write (legibly!) one interesting and little known fact about themselves on their cards.
3. Collect the cards, shuffle them, and distribute one to each participant.
4. Participants take turns reading the card they were given and guessing who wrote it. After one to two guesses, the rest of the group can take a guess or two.

For example . . .	➤ "I have been to 49 of the 50 states. I can't believe the last one I have yet to visit is right in the middle of the country, but it is!"

Tips for	➤ Make sure no one gets his or her own card.
success . . .	➤ Give an example of something to write on the cards only if participants get stuck (and then write something different on your own card).
Try these	➤ Give some parameters to what should be written.
variations . . .	For example, have everyone share their most embarrassing moment, their ideal vacation, or how they would spend a million dollars.
	➤ For groups that don't know each other at all, use this as an icebreaker activity. After a card is read, the owner of that card stands, introduces himself or herself and briefly, elaborates on what is written.
	➤ Divide larger groups up into smaller teams of 8 to 20 members to use this activity.

HA!

This is . . .	➤ A quick activity in which participants try not to laugh while saying "ha" repeatedly.
Use it to . . .	➤ Warm the group up and get members laughing together.
Best group size . . .	➤ Up to about 20.
Materials you'll need . . .	➤ No materials are necessary for this activity.
Here's how . . .	1. Participants sit in a circle.
	2. Announce that one person will say one word to the person on his or her right.
	3. That person will repeat it twice to the person on his or her right.
	4. That next person will repeat the same word three times to the person on his or her right, and so on.
	5. Tell the group to treat this seriously and *not* to laugh.
	6. Then tell the first person the word: ha.
For example . . .	➤ Ha.
	➤ Ha, ha.
	➤ Ha, ha, ha.
	➤ Ha, ha, ha, ha.
	➤ Ha, ha, ha, ha, ha.

| **Tips for** | ➤ Be serious as you set this up. |
| **success . . .** | ➤ Encourage participants to make eye contact as they play (this makes it even more difficult to not laugh). |

Try these	➤ Have the group start over if anyone starts laughing; see if the group can get around the circle without any laughter.
variations . . .	➤ Use other funny words instead of "ha" (tee hee, har, etc.).
	➤ Divide larger groups into smaller teams of 8 to 20 members to use this activity.

QUOTES

This is . . . ➤ A meeting starter in which participants share their favorite quotes with the group.

Use it to . . . ➤ Help the group warm up as well as get to know each other better.

Best group size . . . ➤ Up to about 20.

Materials you'll need . . . ➤ No materials are necessary for this activity.

Here's how . . .
1. Before the meeting, tell participants to bring their favorite quote (either written down or memorized).
2. In the meeting, have participants share their quote and then explain why it is important to them.

For example . . . ➤ " 'To thine own self be true' is my favorite quote. When I was in my early 20s I realized that I was trying to be what others expected or wanted of me. I wasn't happy. When I came to terms with who I am, and then lived true to that, I found great joy as well as inner peace."

Tips for success . . .

➤ You go first to demonstrate how much detail you want them to go into.

➤ It doesn't have to be an actual quote, it could be a "saying" or "words they live by."

Try these variations . . .

➤ Make this more difficult by not giving participants advance warning. Allow them to paraphrase their favorite quote if they can't remember it word for word.

➤ Rather than a quote, have participants share their favorite saying or lesson learned from their parents while growing up.

➤ Divide larger groups up into smaller teams of 8 to 20 members to use this activity.

RUMORS

This is . . .   ➤ An activity in which participants build rumors to-gether.

Use it to . . .   ➤ Warm a group up and get them laughing together.

Best group size . . .   ➤ Up to about 20.

Materials you'll need . . .   ➤ No materials are necessary for this activity.

Here's how . . .
1. Participants sit in a circle.
2. The first person points to someone else and says, "Did you hear about _____ ?"
3. The other participant must respond by saying, "Yes, I heard _____ ," and complete the sentence by elaborating (wildly).
4. That participant then points to someone else and says, "Did you hear about _____ ?" and starting a new topic.
5. Repeat steps 2 through 4.

For example . . .
➤ "Did you hear about the soup today?"
➤ "Yes, I heard it was made with monkey brains and marbles!"
➤ "Did you hear about the boy who could speak 24 languages but couldn't remember his own name on the college entrance exams last year?"

> "Yes, I heard he got into Stanford but only if he agreed to teach Armenian to the football team there."

> "Did you hear about the UFO that landed on my roof last night?"

> "Yes, I heard. . . ."

Tips for success . . .
> Give an example or two before play.
> Discourage participants from "helping" each other. Let them think a moment and be creative on their own. The goal is to be wild, silly, and just have a laugh together.

Try these variations . . .
> Reinforce names with a newer group by requiring participants to start their questions with the other person's name.
> Divide larger groups into smaller teams of 6 to 12 members to use this activity.

SHOW AND TELL

This is . . .   ➤ An activity in which participants bring something to the meeting from their workspace and share its significance with the group.

Use it to . . .   ➤ Help participants get to know each other a little better and warm them up for later.

Best group size . . .   ➤ Up to about 20.

Materials you'll need . . .   ➤ Participants bring one thing from their workspace for this activity.

Here's how . . .

1. Before the meeting, advise all participants to bring something from their office to the meeting (or send them back to their workspace to grab something now).
2. Participants take turns showing what they brought from their workspace and what it means to them.

For example . . .

➤ "Well, I brought this bobblehead figurine of the guy from the TV show "The Office." My kids gave this to me because they say I laugh too hard when I watch that show. Maybe that's because it's so close to how things run around here sometimes!"

➤ "This is a picture of my fiancée. I love him so much, and I keep his picture close because he's in

Iraq right now. We're hoping to get married in 3 months when he gets home, but until I see him and feel him in my arms, I won't be sure."

Tips for success . . .   ➤ Share your item with the group to demonstrate. Keep your explanation quick (unless you have enough time for everyone to take several minutes).

Try these variations . . .

➤ Put all the items in the center, and have participants guess which item belongs to who.

➤ Ban all pictures, so the items they bring must be some kind of object (the conversations can be more fun or challenging this way).

➤ Divide larger groups into smaller teams of 8 to 20 members to use this activity. Alternatively, have all participants mingle with each other, holding what they brought. As they make self-introductions, they explain about their item.

SOUND AND MOVEMENT

This is . . . ➤ An activity in which participants make sounds and movements in a circle and try to remember the sound and movement the others made before them.

Use it to . . . ➤ Get the group energized with physical activity.

Best group size . . . ➤ Up to about 20.

Materials you'll need . . . ➤ No materials are necessary for this activity.

Here's how . . .
1. Participants stand in a circle.
2. You start by making a movement with any part of your body.
3. The person to your right now must mimic this movement and add a movement of his or her own.
4. The next person must mimic the two movements and then add his or her own movement.
5. Continue around the circle until it's your turn again.

6. On your next turn, repeat all the movements, but add a sound to the movement you put into play.

7. Play continues around the circle, with each participant adding a sound to the movement he or she had contributed.

For example . . .
➤ You wave to everyone.
➤ The person on your right, Alejandro, waves to everyone and then blinks his eyes.
➤ The person on Alejandro's right, Ava waves, blinks, and then takes one step backward.
➤ When it's your turn again, you do all the movements that have accumulated, but when you wave, you also say "hello."
➤ Next, Alejandro says "hello" while waving, and then sniffs loudly while he blinks.
➤ Then, Ava says "hello" while waving, sniffs while blinking, and then stomps her foot loudly when she steps backward.

Tips for success . . .
➤ Encourage participants to keep the movements and sounds simple.
➤ No movement or sound may be used a second time. (This puts more pressure on people near the end of the circle.)

Try these variations . . .
➤ Make it more difficult by prohibiting the use of actual words.
➤ Play with just movements, or play with just sounds.
➤ Challenge the group to make the movements flow from person to person.
➤ Divide larger groups into smaller teams of 6 to 12 members to use this activity.

BRAGGING RIGHTS

This is . . .   ➤ An activity in which participants guess something about themselves that may give them bragging rights within the group, and then they test their theory.

Use it to . . .   ➤ Help participants get to know each other better and warm them up for a meeting.

Best group size . . .   ➤ Up to about 20.

Materials you'll need . . .   ➤ Optional: several small prizes.

Here's how . . .

1. Give participants a few minutes to think of something that they can assert is a bragging right for themselves.
2. Each participant will state his or her bragging right.
3. Test the bragging right with the rest of the group.

For example . . .

➤ Chuck submits that he's been to more states (48) than anyone else in the group. A quick show of hands indicates that the next highest is 41.

➤ Mark claims that he has the largest shoe size (13.5) in the group. A quick comparison shows that he is correct.

> Caroline claims she can speak more languages (four) than anyone. Upon review, it is found that David speaks six. But then it is revealed that Caroline *can* speak more non-European languages than anyone and that she has more languages (three) spoken regularly in her home than anyone else.

Tips for success . . .

> If someone fails to identify a bragging right, have the group coax and encourage until he or she thinks of one.

Try these variations . . .

> Give small prizes for each participant who correctly identifies a bragging right.

> Have participants write their bragging rights down. Gather the written statements, and then read them to the group anonymously. Have the group try to guess who made the claim before determining if it's valid or not.

> Divide larger groups into smaller teams of 8 to 12 members to use this activity.

T-SHIRTS

This is . . .	➤ An activity in which participants wear their favorite T-shirt to work and explain, briefly, why it's their favorite.
Use it to . . .	➤ Help participants get to know each other a little better as well as be comfortable at the meeting.
Best group size . . .	➤ Up to about 20.
Materials you'll need . . .	➤ Participants must agree to wear (or bring) their favorite T-shirt to the meeting.
Here's how . . .	1. Participants sit in a circle. 2. Participants take turns telling the group why the T-shirt they are wearing is their favorite.
For example . . .	➤ "I'm Logan. My dad got me this Guinness T-shirt when he was in Ireland. It's my favorite because it's the first time he ever got me something with beer on it, and I guess it represents to me that he was finally acknowledging that I'm a real adult now!"
Tips for success . . .	➤ Tell about your T-shirt first so that participants get a sense for how much time or detail you want from them when it's their turn.

➤ For some groups, you may have to specify up front any moral or decency guidelines that must be followed regarding the content of the T-shirts.

Try these
variations . . .
➤ Participants just bring the T-shirts, not wear them. When it's their turn, they tell about the T-shirt first and then show it.
➤ Use this for an icebreaker activity by having participants introduce themselves before sharing information about their T-shirts.
➤ For larger groups, have participants mingle and use the T-shirts as conversation starters.

TEN FINGERS

This is . . .
➤ An activity in which participants stop holding up fingers as they agree with statements being made.

Use it to . . .
➤ Help a large group get to know each other better.

Best group size . . .
➤ Up to about 20.

Materials you'll need . . .
➤ No materials are necessary for this activity.

Here's how . . .
1. Have everyone sit or stand in a circle and hold up 10 fingers.
2. Each participant will take a turn making a statement that is true of himself or herself.
3. After the statement is made, all who cannot say that the same is true for themselves must lower one finger.
4. Continue play until a participant has lost all of his or her fingers.

For example . . .
➤ "I have a dog."
➤ "I exercise at least three times a week."
➤ "I read a novel last year."
➤ "I did not watch TV last night."

Tips for success . . .	➤ Encourage broader rather than narrower statements. For example, "I can speak a foreign language" rather than "I can speak Japanese."
Try these variations . . .	➤ Allow participants to put their thumb back up when they do share something in common with the others. This will give them two or more chances to stay in the game longer.
	➤ Divide larger groups into smaller teams of 8 to 20 members to use this activity.

TIME CAPSULE

This is . . .	➤ A two-part activity in which participants place items in a box to be opened a year later.
Use it to . . .	➤ Help participants get to know each other as well as to provide reflection a year later.
Best group size . . .	➤ Up to about 20.
Materials you'll need . . .	➤ One large box. ➤ Items that participants bring.
Here's how . . .	1. Before the meeting, instruct participants to bring one piece of memorabilia that is significant to them at this point in their career (or life). It must be something that they can part with (at least for a year!). 2. In the meeting, have participants explain why they brought what they brought. 3. Place all the items into a box. 4. A year later, gather the same participants and open the box. 5. Reflect on what the items meant then and on what they mean now.

For	➤ "I brought this business card for Lauryn Bonner.
example . . .	She's my most promising lead right now, and, if I get an account with her firm, we'll all be celebrating."
	➤ "I want to put in this picture of us at the company picnic last month. I couldn't believe how connected I felt (and do feel!) to all of you."

| **Tips for** | ➤ Announce this activity well in advance, perhaps at |
| **success . . .** | the meeting that happens before this one. |

Try these	➤ Use this activity as a team forms to start a project
variations . . .	with defined beginning and end dates. Fill the box at the beginning of the project, including a note written by participants about their hopes, aspirations, projections, and so forth for the project. At the end of the project, open the box and reflect on what transpired compared with the notes.
	➤ Divide larger groups into smaller teams of 6 to12 members. After each smaller team has filled its time capsule, put all the time capsules into a larger one for the whole group.

WHAT ARE YOU DOING?

This is . . . ➤ An activity in which participants perform simple acts while saying they are doing something else.

Use it to . . . ➤ Warm the group up, laugh, and get physically active.

Best group size . . . ➤ Up to about 20.

Materials you'll need . . . ➤ Optional: a small prize for the winning team.

Here's how . . .

1. Divide the group in half. Stand in lines facing each other.
2. The first participants in each line step forward to face each other.
3. One participant starts by performing a simple act.
4. The second person asks, "What are you doing?" to which the first person says anything *except* what he or she is actually doing.
5. He or she then goes to the end of his or her line and the next person from that line steps forward and asks, "What are you doing?"

6. The second person, having stayed where he or she was, is now performing the action the first person said that he or she was doing. But he or she responds by saying they are doing anything except what they are actually doing and goes to the end of his or her line.
7. Continue until everyone has had a turn.
8. See how fast the group can put all participants through one round.

For example . . .

➤ Adam faces Ruth and acts like he's drinking something. Ruth asks, "What are you doing?" Adam responds, "I'm vacuuming." He then goes to the end of his line, and the next person in his line, Kent, steps forward. Ruth is now vacuuming when Kent asks, "What are you doing?" to which she replies, "I'm playing a video game." She goes to the end of her line, and the next person, Maria, steps forward to ask Kent what he's doing. He is playing a video game but responds otherwise, and so on.

Tips for success . . .

➤ Walk the teams through a couple of rounds before keeping score. Tips on scoring are below.
➤ Don't let any activity be repeated.

Try these variations . . .

➤ Keep score and award a prize to the winning team. Each team starts with 10 points. A point is lost if anyone hesitates more than 3 to 4 seconds or if anyone says what he or she is actually doing. The team that has points remaining after the other one goes to 0 is the winner.
➤ Divide larger groups into smaller teams of 8 to 20 members to use this activity.

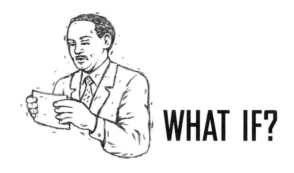

WHAT IF?

This is . . .   ➤ A meeting opener in which participants think about, ask, and then answer hypothetical "what if" questions.

Use it to . . .   ➤ Help a group warm up and have a laugh together.

Best group size . . .   ➤ Up to about 20.

Materials you'll need . . .   ➤ An index card for each participant.
➤ A pen for each participant.

Here's how . . .
1. Participants write a question that begins with "what if" on their card.
2. Everyone passes his or her card to the right.
3. Participants then write their own answer to the question they now have in front of them (the one that was written by the person on their left).
4. Choose a participant to read only the question on his or her card.
5. Next, the person sitting to his or her right reads only the answer on his or her card.
6. Repeat steps 4 and 5 above.

For example . . .   ➤ Lynn wrote the question, "What if we all had a second head?" She passes her card to Patrick, on her right. Patrick answers this question with, "I'd have a lot of trouble deciding what to eat every day!"

➤ Later, Lynn reads the question in front of her, which was written by someone on her left. It says, "What if money grew on trees?" Patrick, who is to Lynn's right, reads his response to the question in front of him, "I'd have a lot of trouble deciding what to eat every day!"

Tips for success . . .
➤ Realize that the answers read will not match the questions read, but that's half the fun!

Try these variations . . .
➤ After step 2, have participants read the question they received and give their answer aloud to the group. This is not as silly, but it allows participants to get to know each other a little better.

➤ Divide larger groups into smaller teams of 8 to 20 members to use this activity.

CHAPTER 5

Activities Best for Large Groups (12 to 40)

The activities in this chapter are designed for larger groups. With larger groups, the challenge is for all the participants to feel engaged and involved without spending too much time doing this during the activity. Therefore, most activities that have participants share or explain something to the rest of the group, like those in Chapter 4, don't work well for these larger groups (unless you break the group up first). The meeting openers in this chapter either have everyone stay in the group together for very brief interactions or require the group to be broken up into pairs, trios, or small teams. Chapter 2 has dozens of ideas on how to divide a group up for these activities.

Although designed primarily for huge groups, most of the meeting openers in Chapters 6 work quite well with medium to large groups. Also, the activities in Chapter 4, although targeted to smaller groups, can also work well with large groups. Just break the group up first. So don't limit yourself to this chapter if you're working with a medium to larger group.

BEACH BALL

This is . . .	➤ An activity in which participants toss a beach ball and answer questions written on the ball when they catch it.
Use it to . . .	➤ Warm a group up and get them moving physically.
Best group size . . .	➤ Up to about 40.
Materials you'll need . . .	➤ A beach ball with provocative questions written all over it.
Here's how . . .	1. Have participants stand in a circle. 2. Toss the beach ball to someone. 3. That participant answers the question closest to his or her right thumb on the ball after catching it. 4. After answering the question, he or she tosses the beach ball to someone else in the circle.
For example . . .	➤ What's your favorite flavor of ice cream? ➤ Who is your hero? ➤ What's the last book you read? ➤ Where did you go to high school? ➤ When did you get your first job? ➤ Where do you keep your bread at home? ➤ Who last saw your bare feet? ➤ When is your next vacation?

Tips for success . . .	➤ Write the questions legibly on the blown up beach ball with a permanent marker, and let the ink dry completely.
	➤ Put one question in each panel or segment of the ball. The question answered is determined by which segment the right thumb is touching at the time of the catch.
	➤ It's okay if participants get the ball more than once, as it is unlikely they will get the same question they already answered. If they do, they pass and just toss the ball on to someone else.
Try these variations . . .	➤ If the group knows each other well, have participants answer the question they get on behalf of the person to their left (or right).
	➤ Make the questions only a choice between two options. For example, Coke or Pepsi, chocolate or vanilla, day or night, beer or wine, book or movie, run or walk, classical or country, play or watch, beach or mountains, and so forth.
	➤ Divide larger groups into smaller teams of 12 to 20 members to use this activity.

BIRTH ORDER

This is . . . ➤ An activity in which participants split into groups depending on their birth order and discuss the pros and cons of their own birth order.

Use it to . . . ➤ Warm the group up and help participants start bonding.

Best group size . . . ➤ Up to about 40.

Materials you'll need . . . ➤ No materials are necessary for this activity.

Here's how . . .
1. Have the group divide up based on their birth order: oldest child, youngest child, middle child (any not oldest or youngest), or only child.
2. Give the teams 5 to 10 minutes to discuss the pros and cons of having their position in their family.
3. Have each team report to the rest of the group what was the best thing about their birth order and what was the worst thing about their birth order.

For example . . . ➤ "The best thing about being in the middle was that we could learn from the mistakes our older siblings made with our parents and adjust. The worst thing was that we often felt invisible as our parents focused on the oldest and the youngest more."

Tips for success . . .
➤ Don't worry if the team sizes are lopsided. As long as each team has more than one member, it can do the activity.
➤ If any team is very large, split it in half and have both teams report out.

Try these variations . . .
➤ Have participants (especially smaller groups) divide themselves by gender and report on the best and worst thing about growing up male or female.
➤ Have participants divide themselves by number of children they have—one, many, or none—and report on the best and worst thing about having that many children.
➤ Have participants divide themselves by marital status—married, widowed, divorced, not married, partnered—and report on the best and worst thing about each status.

CHEERLEADERS

This is . . . ➤ An activity in which participants create a short cheer to relate to the meeting's topic.

Use it to . . . ➤ Help participants warm up, relax, and let go of inhibitions.

Best group size . . . ➤ Up to about 40.

Materials you'll need . . . ➤ Optional: a small prize for the winning team.

Here's how . . .
1. Divide the group into teams of four to eight members.
2. Give each team 5 minutes to create and practice a cheer. The cheer should be related to the organization, the meeting issue(s), or some other relevant topic declared up front. The cheer should last only 1 minute (or less).
3. Have each of the teams perform its cheer for the rest of the group.

For example . . . ➤ The cheerleaders take turns saying "boom" 21 times for a 21 gun salute. Then they shout together: "Give me an *I!* Give me a *T!* Give me a *2!* Give me a *1!* What's that spell? *IT21!* Let's hear it for the IT-21st Century Project!"

Tips for success . . .

➤ Encourage teams to be creative and include all members when doing the cheer.

➤ Supply some pom-poms to be used in the cheers.

Try these variations . . .

➤ Use the cheers to celebrate success. The cheers can be about something that is going well in the organization, or something that went well on a project, or even someone who did an exceptional job.

➤ Have a cheer contest. Participants can vote, independent of their team members, for any cheering team except their own. Award a prize to the best cheering squad.

DRAG QUEEN NAMES

This is . . .	➤ An activity in which participants make up new names for themselves following a general rule of thumb that drag queens sometimes use.
Use it to . . .	➤ Warm the group up in a silly way.
Best group size . . .	➤ Up to about 40.
Materials you'll need . . .	➤ No materials are necessary for this activity.
Here's how . . .	1. Have the group sit in a circle.
	2. Explain that a way to rename oneself is to take the name of one's first pet and pair it with the name of the street one lived on as a kid.
	3. Give the group a few minutes to create their new names
	4. Go around the circle sharing names (and stories that go with them!).
For example . . .	➤ "Well, I guess my name would be Greta Belfield. My first pet was a beautiful dog Greta. We got her when I was in middle school. I used to sleep with her every night! Anyway, we also lived on Belfield Drive, where I grew up in Ohio."
	➤ "My new name would be Ernie Farwell. Hmm, that doesn't sound very fun! Anyway, Ernie was

our pet mouse. I don't even remember our house on Farwell, but it was in Chicago, before we moved out to the suburbs when I was very young."

Tips for success . . .

➤ Be prepared to share your name first, to show how it's done.

➤ If participants have never had a pet, perhaps they can use the name of their favorite stuffed animal, their first car, or anything else they gave a name to when they were younger. Alternatively, maybe their street name is good for a single name (like RuPaul!).

Try these variations . . .

➤ Use current pet's names and current street names.

➤ Have participants think of screen names they'd use if they were movie stars. Give them freedom to choose any name, and then have them tell how they chose the one they did.

➤ Divide larger groups into smaller teams of 8 to 20 members to use this activity.

 # EDITOR

This is . . .	➤ An activity in which participants modify a newspaper article to create a completely different story.
Use it to . . .	➤ Warm up a group and get the team working together.
Best group size . . .	➤ Up to about 40.
Materials you'll need . . .	➤ A very short newspaper article for each team. ➤ A pen for each team.

Here's how . . .

1. Divide the group into small teams of two to four members.
2. Give each team a newspaper article.
3. Teams have 5 minutes to edit the article to create a different story altogether.
4. Share the stories with the rest of the group for a good laugh.

For example . . .

➤ Columbus, October 29—The Mexican vacation was ~~supposed to be~~ free for ~~dozens of~~ Columbus-area residents.~~ But they paid the price~~ when they went to prison ~~for smuggling drugs home in their sneakers~~.

> Most were ~~in their early 20s,~~ recruited by ~~members of an international drug ring that shipped cocaine from the Central American country of Belize to Columbus by way of~~ Houston.

> The lure was ~~an all-expenses-paid vacation to Chetumal, Mexico, and~~ $1, 000 cash when they returned home.

Tips for success . . .

> Use short newspaper articles of three to five paragraphs (longer articles would make the activity drag out too long).

> Editing consists of only deleting words—no words may be altered, added, or rearranged (see the example above).

Try these variations . . .

> For smaller groups, give all the teams the same article and have them compete for the most clever edit. For this variation, a slightly longer article works better.

> Allow up to a certain number of additional words to be included in the edits.

> For larger groups, conduct the activity as above but either skip step 4 or limit step 4 to include only two to three neighboring teams.

LINE

This is . . . ➤ An activity in which participants in small groups try to guess the length of a line.

Use it to . . . ➤ Warm up a group, get members talking, and provide some fun.

Best group size . . . ➤ Up to about 40.

Materials you'll need . . .
➤ A long piece of rope or some masking tape to make a long line on the floor or a wall.
➤ One pen and one piece of paper for each team.
➤ A small prize.

Here's how . . .
1. Before the activity begins, lay a long piece of rope on the floor. Alternatively, make a long line on the floor using masking tape.
2. Divide the group into smaller teams of four to eight members.
3. Give the teams 5 minutes to guess exactly how long the line is.
4. Award a prize for the closest guess.

Tips for success . . .
➤ Make the line long (30 to 50 feet), but make it an uneven length (e.g., 32 feet and 4.5 inches).
➤ Announce that the line may not be touched or moved by anyone.

> Have the teams write down their guess before the sharing begins (to prevent any overly competitive people from changing their guess after hearing other teams).

> Short of using a ruler or other exact measuring devise, the teams may use any means to determine the length.

Try these variations . . .

> Have the rope curvy rather than pulled in a straight line.

> Rather than a rope, use beans in a jar (but be sure to count them first!). The teams try to guess how many beans.

> For large groups, have several ropes, and see which team guesses closest for any or all of them.

NEW HANDSHAKES

This is . . .   ➤ An activity in which participants work in teams to create handshakes or greetings for the group.

Use it to . . .   ➤ Warm the group up and give them something that will continue to pay off throughout the meeting. This is especially good for meetings that will last all day or longer.

Best group size . . .   ➤ Up to about 40.

Materials you'll need . . .   ➤ No materials are necessary for this activity.

Here's how . . .   1. Divide the group into three teams of roughly equal size.
2. Team 1 will create a unique handshake or greeting to use when meeting others. All group members will use this when meeting each other for the first time. The message should be, "Welcome. I'm happy to make your acquaintance, and I look forward to working with you."
3. Team 2 will create a handshake or greeting for congratulating others. All group members will use this to acknowledge and recognize when someone does something well (much like the "high five" is used by many now).

4. Team 3 will create a handshake or greeting for encouraging others. All group members will use this to support or strengthen another member.
5. After 5 minutes, have each team teach the new handshake or greeting to the rest of the group.
6. Encourage the group to use the new handshakes and greetings whenever appropriate throughout the meeting.

Tips for success . . .

➤ The teams do not have to be exactly equal size, so don't spend too much time or energy splitting them up.

➤ Depending on the group, you may have to explicitly remind participants to keep their handshakes or greetings business-appropriate.

Try these variations . . .

➤ Don't give the groups time to teach the new handshake/greeting. Tell them to just start using the one they created whenever appropriate. Others will learn as they see it used.

➤ Rather than having each team teach their new handshake/greeting to the whole group, have the teams disperse and mingle among themselves, teaching each other one on one.

➤ Delete or add handshakes/greetings to meet the needs of your group. Consider a handshake/greeting for thanking, for energizing, for reconnecting after conflict, and so forth.

NEW WORDS

This is . . .   ➤ An activity in which participants create a useful new word together.

Use it to . . .   ➤ Help the group warm up, especially if smaller teams will be used later in the meeting.

Best group size . . .   ➤ Up to about 40.

Materials you'll need . . .   ➤ Optional: a small prize for the winning team.

Here's how . . .

1. Divide the group into teams of four to six members.
2. Give the teams 5 minutes to each create a new word (including spelling) that would be a useful addition to the English language, especially at your organization.
3. Have the teams share their new words with the rest of the group.

For example . . .   ➤ "Our new word is *superdupe.* This is the word used to describe how duped you feel when you go to the cafeteria and get all excited about their soup of the day, only to get to the front of the line and find that they ran out . . . again . . . already! So, you might say, 'I was superduped at the cafeteria today' or 'That client superduped me when he led me on like that for so long.' "

Tips for success . . .

➤ Don't give teams too much help or too many suggestions, or they may feel bound to follow your lead rather than be creative together.

Try these variations . . .

➤ Vote on the best new word, and award a prize to the winning team. Participants can vote independently for any new word except the one their team created (otherwise everyone may vote for their own and create a huge tie!).

PHOTO
SCAVENGER HUNT

This is . . .   ➤ An activity in which participants collect a few pictures on a cell phone.

Use it to . . .   ➤ Get smaller teams working together and moving around physically.

Best group size . . .   ➤ Up to about 20.

Materials you'll need . . .
➤ A short list of items to be photographed.
➤ Several members of the group must have cell phones that can take pictures.
➤ A small prize for the winning team.

Here's how . . .
1. Divide the group into teams of four to six members.
2. Make sure each team has at least one cell phone that can take pictures.
3. Allow 5 minutes to take pictures of the items on their list.
4. The first team to take all the pictures wins a small prize.

For example . . .
➤ A picture of someone jumping.
➤ A picture of a chair balancing some way other than on its four legs.

> ➤ A picture of water.
> ➤ A picture of three items that begin with the letter B.

Tips for success . . .
> ➤ None of a team's pictures can be of its own teammates or items that it owns.
> ➤ Keep the list short (four to eight items) for a quick activity.
> ➤ Post the list on a flip chart rather than making copies to distribute.

Try these variations . . .
> ➤ Make the list include people's names in the group.
> ➤ Make it more difficult by requiring the pictures be taken in order.

PORTRAITS

This is . . . ➤ An activity in which participants draw a picture of their partner and then try to guess who is who in all the portraits.

Use it to . . . ➤ Warm the group up and have some creative fun.

Best group size . . . ➤ Up to about 40.

Materials you'll need . . .
➤ One piece of paper for each participant.
➤ Enough markers, crayons, and/or pens for each participant to have several.

Here's how . . .
1. Participants pair up.
2. Give them each a piece of paper and some markers.
3. Allow 5 minutes for them to draw a portrait of their partner. Do not allow portraits to be shown to anyone yet.
4. Gather the drawings.
5. With the group back together, hold up the portraits one by one, and have participants try to guess who is in each one.

Tips for success . . .
➤ Give the artist only a very short time to explain or elaborate on his or her drawing.
➤ Encourage those who claim they can't draw. The picture doesn't have to be like a photo. Remind

them of Picasso and other artists who drew inter-
pretations of their subjects, not exact replicas.

Try these
variations . . .
➤ After step 4, shuffle the portraits and randomly
hand them out to everyone. Make sure no one
gets the portrait that he or she drew. Then have
everyone mingle and try to find the person who
fits the portrait he or she has.
➤ Give the portraits to their subjects and allow the
subjects to add to (or take away from) the portrait.
In the group, subjects show their portrait and explain why they altered it (or not).
➤ Have all participants draw the same subject (you?
your organization's leader?).
➤ Divide larger groups into smaller groups of 12 to
24 members, and have each of the smaller groups
follow steps 1 through 5.

SWAP

This is . . . ➤ An activity in which people call out names and swap places in a circle.

Use it to . . . ➤ Energize the group before a difficult meeting or midway through a long meeting.

Best group size . . . ➤ Up to about 40.

Materials you'll need . . . ➤ No materials are necessary for this activity.

Here's how . . .
1. Participants stand in a circle. You stand in the middle as "it."
2. All participants bow their heads.
3. On your signal, participants look up and then look at someone else in the circle.
4. If they do not make eye contact with the person they look at (he or she is looking at someone else), they do nothing.
5. When two people do make eye contact, they scream and quickly swap places.
6. While they are swapping places you, "it," try to capture one of their vacancies.
7. Whoever is left without a spot in the circle is "it" for the next round.
8. Repeat several times.

For example . . .	➤ Lynn looked up and saw Derrick, but he was not looking at her, so she stayed put.
	➤ When Derrick looked up, however, he made eye contact with Julio. They both scream and swap places.
	➤ Meanwhile, Nikki and Bill also made eye contact and are also racing across the circle to swap places.
Tips for success . . .	➤ Participants should not swap with the same person more than once.
Try these variations . . .	➤ For new groups, this would be a good activity to play after an introduction activity. Have the pairs who make eye contact scream each other's names before they swap.
	➤ Require that all participants not touch each other (no bumping into others) as they are swapping places. This will make it much more difficult to swap places.
	➤ For a larger group, make two or more circles of 20 to 30 participants each.

UNUSUAL COMMONALITIES

This is . . .	➤ A meeting opener in which participants discover what they have in common with each other.
Use it to . . .	➤ Get participants warmed up and connecting with each other.
Best group size . . .	➤ Up to about 40.
Materials you'll need . . .	➤ Optional: two small prizes for the winning pair.
Here's how . . .	1. Have participants pair up. 2. Give them 2 minutes to find things they have in common. 3. Give them 1 more minute to determine the most *unusual* thing they have in common. 4. Have the pairs share their unusual commonalities with the group.
For example . . .	➤ "Of all the things Jessie and I have in common, the most unusual is that at our age, neither of us has ever tasted one drop of alcohol in our lives!" ➤ "This is not a happy thing, but both Jose and I were widowed before we were 40 years old."

> "Not only have Chris and I both been to Japan, but we were actually there at the same time without knowing it!"

Tips for success . . .
> Encourage participants to pair up with someone they don't know.

Try these variations . . .
> Make the task more difficult by putting participants in groups of three or four members rather than in pairs.
> Award small prizes for the pair with the most unusual commonality.
> With small groups, see if the entire group can find one unusual thing they all have in common.
> After the pairs have found the most unusual commonality, have them find another pair to work with, and repeat the process in their new group of four.

WHO ELSE?

This is . . .   ➤ An activity in which participants change places with each other in the circle based on information that is true of themselves.

Use it to . . .   ➤ Warm participants up and get them energized by some physical activity.

Best group size . . .   ➤ Up to about 40.

Materials you'll need . . .   ➤ No materials are necessary for this activity.

Here's how . . .
1. Select one person to be "it" first.
2. Everyone else sits in a circle.
3. "It" stands in the middle and states something that is true of himself or herself and then asks, "Who else?"
4. Immediately, anyone in the group for whom the statement is also true must jump up and find a new seat. "It" also tries to occupy one of the vacated seats.
5. The person left without a seat is the new "it."
6. Repeat steps 3 through 5.

For example . . .   ➤ "I love to make chocolate chip cookies at home."
➤ "I have been to Canada."

> "I know all the words to the national anthem."
> "I watch at least a little TV everyday."

Tips for success . . .
> You be the first "it" to show how the game is played.
> If the person who was "it" doesn't secure a seat, he or she is "it" again for the next round.
> Be sure the playing area is free of obstructions or hazards.
> Make adjustments if a participant has a physical condition that would inhibit his or her participation.

Try these variations . . .
> It's tempting to make vague, general statements true of everyone to encourage more empty seats. Give a prize to the "it" who makes fewer than X number of people move and still gets a seat for himself or herself.
> For smaller groups that don't want the physical activity, play around a large table. All participants have one ball, spoon, or other small item. When a statement is true of them, participants place their item on the table and then pick up a different item. Simultaneously, the person who's "it" also attempts to claim an item.
> Allow "it" to call out "Well, *who else?*" without first making a statement. When "it" does this, everyone in the circle must change seats.

CHAPTER 6

Activities Best for Huge Groups (Up to a Billion)

The activities in this chapter are best for huge groups: over 40 people. Think company-wide meetings, large hotel ballrooms, you get the picture. It's impractical to try to get everyone to know each other well or even to get everyone introduced to each other. A realistic objective is to get everyone to meet or get to know a few people better. These activities do just that. Most of them require people to either mingle (with definite structure to the mingling) or be divided up into smaller teams. Chapter 2 has dozens of ideas on how to divide a group up for these activities.

The activities in Chapters 4 and 5 are designed for smaller groups, but don't count all of them out for a huge group. Most of them can work for a huge group as long as you break the group up into smaller teams first.

 ALPHABET LETTERS

This is . . .	➤ An activity in which participants form letters in small teams as they are called out.
Use it to . . .	➤ Get a group warmed up and physically active.
Best group size . . .	➤ Unlimited.
Materials you'll need . . .	➤ No materials are necessary for this activity.

Here's how . . .

1. Have the group form teams of four to six participants.
2. Call out any letter from the alphabet.
3. Teams must form the letter with their bodies.
4. Repeat steps 2 through 4.

For example . . .

➤ The letter A was called. Chris forms one side of the A; Terry forms the other. Cary and Jim together form the cross line.

➤ Marianna and Laura form the top part of the A, Iona and Ishita form the lower legs and bend at their waist to form the cross line.

Tips for success . . .

➤ All members of the team must be part of the letter. Even the letter I will have more than one person involved.

> Start with easier letters first (A, E, T, and other letters with straight lines only) until they get the hang of it.

Try these
variations . . .
> Include numbers and other symbols on a standard keyboard (@, $, %, &, etc.).
> With smaller groups, have them do it in pairs. This will make it more difficult.

A B C D ALPHABET SEARCH

This is . . .   ➤ An activity in which participants try to identify 26 things among themselves, each item beginning with a different letter of the alphabet.

Use it to . . .   ➤ Warm the group up and get smaller teams working together.

Best group size . . .   ➤ Unlimited.

Materials you'll need . . .   ➤ No materials are necessary for this activity.

Here's how . . .
1. Divide the group into teams of four to six members.
2. Each team needs to find among themselves 26 items that start with all 26 letters of the alphabet A through Z.

For example . . .   ➤ The team has among them an *A*rizona driver license, a *b*allpoint pen, a *c*redit card, a *d*ollar, an *e*nvelope, a *f*ive-dollar bill, and so forth.

Tips for success . . .   ➤ The winning team is the one that gets its 26 items first or the one that gets closest to 26.
➤ Decide how creative the teams can be with their letters. For example, can Benjamin's sock be used for B?

➤ Decide if items can be used twice. For example, can a VISA credit card be used for the V as well as the C?

Try these
variations . . .

➤ Send the teams on a scavenger hunt to gather the 26 items. Nothing presented can be anything that they had between them to start.

ALWAYS AND NEVER

This is . . .	➤ An activity in which participants make absolute statements to each other based on topics given to them.
Use it to . . .	➤ Warm a group up and help participants get to know each other better.
Best group size . . .	➤ Unlimited.
Materials you'll need . . .	➤ No materials are necessary for this activity.
Here's how . . .	1. Have the group wander around in a large space.
	2. When you give the signal, participants stop and pair up with the person closest to them.
	3. You announce a topic.
	4. The first person in the pair must make a statement about the topic that is *always* true for himself or herself.
	5. The second person then makes a statement about the same topic that is *never* true for himself or herself.
	6. After 30 seconds, give the signal for the group to resume wandering around.
	7. Repeat steps 1 through 6.

For example . . .	➤ Topics may include weather, entertainment, sports, food, current events, travel, animals, education, family, competitors of your organization's, health, and so forth.
	➤ Weather: I *always* bring an umbrella when it looks like rain.
	➤ Weather: I *never* drive in the snow if I don't have to.
Tips for success . . .	➤ Pick a topic at random, and give examples of both statements so that participants can see how easy it is to think them up.
	➤ It's okay to use the same topic more than once (the participants will be with different partners if you use the topic again).
Try these variations . . .	➤ Rather than taking turns with *always* and *never,* announce to the group which statements both participants will make as you announce the topic.
	➤ Have participants decide at the beginning whether all their statements will be *always* or *never* and then stick to that throughout the activity.
	➤ Have both partners say an *always* statement and then both say a *never* statement.

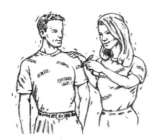

AUTOGRAPH HOUND

This is . . . ➤ An activity in which participants mingle about signing each other's T-shirts as if they were high school yearbooks.

Use it to . . . ➤ Help the group warm up or even to close out a project or other significant piece of work participants just accomplished.

Best group size . . . ➤ Unlimited.

Materials you'll need . . . ➤ One oversized, white T-shirt for each participant.
➤ A marker for each participant.

Here's how . . .
1. Give everyone a T-shirt and ask them to put it on. They can go change, or they can put it on over their clothing.
2. Give everyone a marker.
3. The participants mingle. They both autograph other participants' shirts and gather autographs on their own.

For example . . . ➤ Great job with the cost analysis!—Benjamin.
➤ BYOC (bring your own chocolate) next time we work a weekend together!—Miriam.

Tips for
success . . .

- ➤ If participants opt to wear the T-shirt over their clothing, be sure to use water-based markers. If the ink bleeds through, their clothing will not likely be ruined.
- ➤ Make sure you have T-shirts that will fit everyone, even the larger participants. Too big is always better than too small.
- ➤ Encourage the participants to write a few words beyond just their name.
- ➤ Rather than supplying T-shirts, you may want to have everyone bring an old one of their own that they won't mind getting "messed up."

Try these
variations . . .

- ➤ Make the activity an icebreaker, and collect only signatures. See who can collect the most in a limited amount of time.
- ➤ Make the activity an icebreaker, and collect only signatures. Keep going until every participant has collected a signature from everyone in the group.
- ➤ Use T-shirts that mean something; for example, they have the organization's logo or the project's slogan.
- ➤ Give different colored T-shirts to different teams within the group. Have them gather signatures either from their own team members only or from all group participants.
- ➤ Use small pads of paper instead of the T-shirts, as if they were high school yearbooks.

BEST OF TIMES

This is . . .	➤ An activity in which participants share the best thing that's happened to them in the past week.
Use it to . . .	➤ Warm the group up and get participants connecting with others.
Best group size . . .	➤ Unlimited.
Materials you'll need . . .	➤ No materials are necessary for this activity.
Here's how . . .	1. Have the participants each think (silently) of the best thing that has happened to them within the past week. 2. Have the group mingle. As participants meet each other, they introduce themselves and then share their best thing from the past week.
For example . . .	➤ "My name is Nikki. Just 2 days ago my brother came home for a short visit and brought his 3-year-old daughter with him. I just love playing with that little cutie!" ➤ "My name is Alejandro. Last night my daughter made homemade chocolate chip cookies. Mmmmm!"

Tips for success . . .

➤ As the participants mingle, it's okay if they form pairs or trios to share their stories. The goal is to be discussing rather than looking for someone to talk with.

➤ Share your story with the group first to demonstrate how quick and easy it is and that the stories don't have to be terribly significant.

➤ Have participants limit their story exchanges to 90 seconds. It's about quantity over quality at this point. (Encourage them to get into more depth with those they want to during the break or some other time.)

Try these variations . . .

➤ Have the participants also share "worst" stories. Use this to help them to get some gripes off their mind before diving into the meeting at hand.

➤ Expand (a month? a year?) the time frame, or shrink it (24 hours? since waking up today?).

➤ Limit the scope. Rather than the best thing in life, limit it to the best thing at work, to the best thing on the project so far, and so forth.

BLACK JACK

This is . . . ➤ An activity in which participants swap playing cards in an effort to collect exactly 21 points.

Use it to . . . ➤ Help participants break the ice, solve problems, and have fun together competitively.

Best group size . . . ➤ Unlimited.

Materials you'll need . . . ➤ Enough playing cards so that there are some extras left after each participant is given three cards.
➤ Optional: a small prize.

Here's how . . .
1. Shuffle all the cards, and give three cards to each participant.
2. Participants look at their cards (and can show others, if they choose).
3. The object is for participants to trade their cards to form a hand in which the points add up to exactly 21.
4. Participants may not refuse to trade with anyone, but they can decide which card(s) to trade.
5. Once a participant gets 21 points, he or she may exit play and sit down.

For example . . . ➤ Tim's hand is a Jack, Queen, and 5. He needs to eliminate four points. He could trade the Queen for a 6, or the Jack for a 2 and a 4, or the 5 for an Ace.

Tips for success . . .

- The Ace can be 1 point or 11 points depending on what value helps the holder of that card.
- Players can trade one card for two or more cards if the other party is willing.
- If players get stuck, allow them to discard one card and draw another one from the extra cards you hold.
- You may want to give a prize to the first person to get 21 points.
- Require that everyone must make at least one trade before sitting down. This way, those who might be dealt 21 points won't be left out of the interaction.

Try these variations . . .

- Make the activity last longer. Give participants seven cards. The object is for each participant to collect exactly 40 points.
- Award a special prize for anyone who makes their 21 points with two Black Jacks and an Ace.
- Make this an introduction activity by requiring trading partners to introduce themselves to each other before the trade and then shake hands afterward.
- Make it more difficult by requiring the participants to trade blindly. Rather than negotiating what the trade is, both parties choose the card they want to get rid of and swap with each other. Alternatively, have participants draw from the other person's hand any card, hoping it will help them.

BLUE RIBBONS

This is . . .   ➤ An activity in which participants predict their contribution to the meeting's success.

Use it to . . .   ➤ Get the group warmed up and the participants prepared to contribute to the meeting's success.

Best group size . . .   ➤ Unlimited.

Materials you'll need . . .
➤ A blue ribbon for each participant.
➤ A safety pin for each participant (or a roll of tape).
➤ Plenty of dark-colored markers.

Here's how . . .
1. As participants arrive, give them a blue ribbon and a marker.
2. Have participants write their name on their ribbon. Then ask them to also write on the ribbon one contribution they plan to make toward the good of the meeting, for which they will deserve a blue ribbon.
3. Participants then pin on their blue ribbon and mingle with the others, encouraging everyone to "earn" the blue ribbon they are wearing.

For example . . .
➤ For outstanding questions to challenge the status quo.
➤ For restraint in dominating the discussion.
➤ For building bridges among conflicting parties.

Tips for **success . . .**	➤ If you can't find blue ribbons to purchase, you can make them easily out of blue construction paper. Paper ribbons can be "pinned on" with tape.
	➤ Encourage participants to think for themselves and not copy others' contribution ideas.
Try these **variations . . .**	➤ For participants who know each other well, have them pair up and write contributions for their partners. The contribution becomes a challenge to the partner to fulfill during the meeting.
	➤ Use blue ribbons at the end of the meeting to recognize participants for their contributions. Have participants make blue ribbons for each other or for themselves.
	➤ Have participants create the blue ribbons at the beginning of the meeting and then keep them private. After the meeting, have participants reveal their blue ribbon and comment briefly on their success.

CUPS

This is . . .	➤ An activity in which participants use a paper cup to indicate how they feel about the meeting, project, task, or other similar topic.
Use it to . . .	➤ Surface concerns about the project or meeting and have some fun.
Best group size . . .	➤ Unlimited.
Materials you'll need . . .	➤ One paper cup for each participant.
Here's how . . .	1. Distribute one cup to each participant. 2. Allow 3 minutes for participants to do something to the paper cup that represents how they feel about the assigned topic (meeting, project, etc.). 3. Participants mingle and show their cups to each other.
For example . . .	➤ "Sometimes it feels like we pour so much energy and effort into meetings, but then we come out with very little. That's why I poked this hole in the bottom of the cup. It's like we lose so much unnecessarily."
Tips for success . . .	➤ Don't give them too many ideas about what to do to the cup. Let them be creative on their own.

> Discourage anyone from disagreeing or arguing with a participant as he or she explains his or her cup.

> Have a few extra cups on hand (sometimes participants may get out of hand with their frustrations!).

Try these variations . . .

> For smaller groups, have participants sit in a circle and take turns explaining their cup to the whole group.

> Allow other props to be used with the paper cup (pencil, string, tape, etc.).

DANCE CARDS

This is . . .	➤ A mingling activity in which participants make "dates" with each other for when they will chat later.
Use it to . . .	➤ Help participants get to know each other better.
Best group size . . .	➤ Unlimited.
Materials you'll need . . .	➤ An index card for each participant. ➤ A pen for each participant.
Here's how . . .	1. Have participants write numbers 1 through 5 on their card. 2. Participants mingle to fill their card with a name for each number. 3. Upon meeting, participants find a matching open number on their cards and then write each other's name next to the number. 4. Continue until everyone has a name next to each number. Everyone's name will also be on each of those people's cards. 5. After everyone's card is full, call out a number on the card. 6. Participants find the person whose name is at that number on their card and have 1 minute to chat and get to know that person. 7. Call another number on the card and repeat.

For example . . .	➤ Tim's card is empty, but John already has someone on his card at space number 1, so Tim will write John's name in his number 2 spot. John will write Tim's name in his number 2 spot. Now John still needs names for numbers 3 through 5, and Tim still needs to find someone for 1 and 3 through 5. Later, when the number 2 is called, Tim and John will find each other again and talk.
Tips for success . . .	➤ Remind participants that they might not fill their dance card in order, because the number they write for the other person must be the same number that he or she writes for them(see the example above).
	➤ Encourage participants to fill their dance cards quickly. They will have time to visit and get to know each other later.
Try these variations . . .	➤ Rather than performing the activity all at once, have the participants fill their dance cards and then start the meeting. At a good stopping point in the meeting, call out a number. After a minute or two of discussion, go back to the meeting. Later, call out another number, and so on.
	➤ For longer meetings and/or with larger groups, use a paper plate. Divide the plate to look like a clock with 12 numbers. Have participants gather 12 names.

DELEGATION

This is . . . ➤ An activity in which participants are sent off to accomplish tasks delegated to them by their team leader.

Use it to . . . ➤ Get the group interacting and thinking of others positively.

Best group size . . . ➤ Unlimited.

Materials you'll need . . . ➤ No materials are necessary for this activity.

Here's how . . .

1. Divide the group into teams of four to six members. Teams don't have to be exactly the same size.
2. Choose one person on each team to be the Delegator. The rest of the team members are Delegatees.
3. The Delegator then assigns one task to each Delegatee. Tasks are things the Delegatee must do for someone else in the group, not within his or her own team.
4. After a few minutes, the Delegatees go do the Delegator's bidding.

For example . . .
➤ Greet and shake hands with 16 people.
➤ Give two people a 30-second shoulder rub.

- Make eye contact with and smile at everyone in the room.
- Tell four people you hope they win the lottery this week.
- Give two people a note expressing your confidence in them.

Tips for success . . .
- Tasks should be positive and promote happiness, laughter, peace, calm, reassurance, confidence, or some other positive feeling in the group.
- Offer a few, varied examples of ideas for the Delegators but not too many. Otherwise, they will get too locked into your suggestions and not be creative themselves.
- Challenge the Delegatees to deliver their service as cheerfully and eagerly as possible.

Try these variations . . .
- Do another round with someone else on the team as the Delegator. Encourage even more creativity with the second round.
- Have participants pair up. One is Delegator; one is Delegatee. After the Delegatee has performed his or her task, return to the Delegator and switch roles.
- Rather than Delegation, play Consensus. Each team comes to a consensus on what they all (there is no Delegator now) will do to promote a positive environment at the start of the meeting.

DOMINOS

This is . . .	➤ An activity in which participants use dominos to form themselves into groups for seating at tables.
Use it to . . .	➤ Divide especially larger groups into smaller groups.
Best group size . . .	➤ Unlimited.
Materials you'll need . . .	➤ One domino for each participant. ➤ A bag to hold the dominos.
Here's how . . .	1. Each participant randomly picks a domino out of the bag. 2. Have participants form groups of eight (or however many you want seated at a table). 3. All members of the group formed must be connected with one another via the number of dots on one or both ends of their dominos. 4. Once they have made the links, they may be seated at a table (together) for the rest of the meeting.
For example . . .	➤ Each domino has two halves with a set of dots (sometimes both are the same number) on each end. Participants can connect to each other with either number. ➤ A person with a 1/4 domino can connect with someone who has a 4/3 domino (the 4's match).

They can then connect with someone with a 4/4 domino. This person goes in the middle (so the 4's all match). Then they look for someone who has a 1 (to match the first person's 1/4 domino) or a 3 (to match the second person's 4/3 domino), or a 4 (branching off the third person's 4/4 domino).

Tips for success . . .
- ➤ Put a time limit on the activity to push people to group themselves quickly.
- ➤ Before the activity begins, review the possibilities for connecting dots. Especially point out that some dominos have the same number of dots at both ends, making it harder for them to connect with others.

Try these variations . . .
- ➤ After everyone has grouped once, repeat the activity. Have them keep their domino but form another group (the same size or not, as you direct) with different people.
- ➤ After everyone has formed the group size you directed, have them use an icebreaker activity to facilitate introductions with each other at their table.
- ➤ Give everyone two dominos, and direct that both dominos must be used in the connecting. Alternatively, only one domino is used for the first round, and the other is used in a second round later on.

HITCHHIKER

This is . . .   ➤ An activity in which participants sit in fours and mimic their hitchhiker.

Use it to . . .   ➤ Get group members to intermix and become physically involved.

Best group size . . .   ➤ Unlimited.

Materials you'll need . . .   ➤ No materials are necessary for this activity.

Here's how . . .
1. Divide the group into teams of four members.
2. Have teams seat themselves together as if they were in a car (two rows of two). One person is designated "driver."
3. Give the signal, and the driver leaves the vehicle. The remaining passengers move up in their chairs (with someone new becoming the driver).
4. The ex-drivers now join a new vehicle and sit in the vacated back seat. They have become the hitchhiker.
5. The hitchhiker starts doing some action and/or sound.
6. The others in the vehicle must copy him or her exactly.
7. After a moment, give another signal.
8. Repeat steps 3 through 7 several times.

For example . . .	➤ Kelly joins the vehicle and starts whistling. Everyone in the vehicle whistles with her. The signal is given, and the driver leaves. The passengers all move up, and now Jasper is the driver. Jaime has joined as the hitchhiker and starts tapping his foot. All the passengers tap their foot with Jaime. The signal is given again, and Jasper leaves the vehicle to join another one. As Jasper sits down in the new vehicle, he starts yawning. Everyone in Jasper's vehicle starts yawning with him.
Tips for success . . .	➤ Walk two vehicles through the process once so everyone can see how it works.
	➤ Don't wait too long to stop the action again after the hitchhikers get into place. Keep things moving quickly.
Try these variations . . .	➤ Have the passengers continue doing what the last hitchhiker started when the next one joins them. Each hitchhiker builds on what the last one created so that soon the vehicle has its riders performing many things simultaneously.

 HOT SEAT

This is . . . ➤ An activity in which participants ask each other questions to reveal more about themselves.

Use it to . . . ➤ Warm the group up, especially if smaller teams will be working together.

Best group size . . . ➤ Unlimited.

Materials you'll need . . .
➤ Three index cards for each participant.
➤ A pen for each participant.
➤ One die for each team.

Here's how . . .

1. Divide the group into teams of five to eight members.
2. Give participants 3 minutes to write a different question on each of their three index cards.
3. Each team collects their own question cards and shuffles them.
4. The first participant picks a card and rolls the die.
5. Team members count the number on the die left or right of the roller (roller's choice), and that person is in the hot seat. He or she must answer the question posed by the roller, who reads it off the card he or she picked up.
6. Pass the die to the left and repeat steps 4 and 5.

For example . . .	➤ Questions should be open-ended and may or may not have to do with work (you should declare up front if there are parameters). Why do you like working here? What is your favorite breakfast? Who's you're hero here at work? What's the best product or service we offer to our clients? What will you do when you retire?
Tips for success . . .	➤ It's okay if participants ask their own question or are asked the question they wrote.
Try these variations . . .	➤ Have teams swap their stacks of question cards for another round.
	➤ Give each participant one token that can be used at any time to bounce the question back to the roller. For example, if the roller asks a question Susan doesn't want to answer, she plays her token. She doesn't have to answer the question, but the roller who posed the question to her does. The token can be used only once, so participants should choose carefully when they use it!

INDEX CARD QUESTIONS

This is . . .	➤ An activity in which participants create one question to pose to others to find out more about them.
Use it to . . .	➤ Stimulate interesting discussion between members who may already know each other well already or as a way to start conversations among perfect strangers.
Best group size . . .	➤ Unlimited.
Materials you'll need . . .	➤ An index card for each participant. ➤ A pen for each participant. ➤ Optional: a small prize for each team.
Here's how . . .	1. Distribute an index card and a pen to each participant. 2. Participants write one question on their index card that they would like to have answered by the others. 3. Have the participants quickly form teams of three members.

4. In their trios, participants ask each other the questions from the index cards. Even the person asking the question answers it for the other two.
5. After 3 minutes, signal for participants to regroup into a new trio with two new people.
6. Repeat steps 4 and 5.

For example . . .
➤ What's your ultimate career goal?
➤ What's your favorite TV show?
➤ How do you like to spend a day off from work?
➤ Do you have any pets?
➤ What would you do if you won the lottery?

Tips for success . . .
➤ Encourage participants to share as much (or as little) as they are comfortable with when answering the question.

Try these variations . . .
➤ After the first round, have the trios combine into teams of six members. After everyone answers each question, have each team choose the best question. Have small prizes ready for the participants who had the best question.
➤ For the first round, have participants pair up. For subsequent rounds, have them form trios, then groups of four, five, and so on.
➤ For smaller groups, have each trio record their answers on a flip chart. Have the other groups see if they can guess what the question was based on only the answers recorded.

JEOPARDY

This is . . . ➤ An icebreaker activity in which participants have an "answer" on their name tag and seek others to determine the appropriate "question."

Use it to . . . ➤ Warm participants up and help them start to get to know each other.

Best group size . . . ➤ Unlimited.

Materials you'll need . . .
➤ A name tag for each participant.
➤ A pen for each participant.
➤ Optional: tokens and small prizes.

Here's how . . .
1. Participants put their name on their name tag.
2. Below their name, participants write an answer to a question about themselves.
3. Participants mingle. As they read the name tags, they try to guess what the question is that leads to the answer given.

For example . . .
➤ Maria. 23.
➤ "How old you are? How many years have you been married? How many grandchildren do you have?"
➤ "No, the correct question is, 'How many more days till I go on vacation to Ireland?' "

| **Tips for** | ➤ Responses must be in the form of a question. |
| **success . . .** | ➤ Allow three questions before the correct questions are revealed and the pairs mingle again. |

Try these	➤ Declare up front a category for the answers on the
variations . . .	name tags (family, leisure, work, etc.).
	➤ Have participants collect tokens for each right question they guess, and give prizes to winners.
	➤ Leave the names off. Names are given after the participant correctly guesses the question.

MAGNETS

This is . . .   ➤ An activity in which participants quickly try to stand next to one participant while avoiding another one.

Use it to . . .   ➤ Get the group moving and energized.

Best group size . . .   ➤ Unlimited.

Materials you'll need . . .   ➤ No materials are necessary for this activity.

Here's how . . .
1. Have each participant secretly identify two other people in the room and designate one as "A" and one as "R." It doesn't matter who they choose as long as they don't tell anyone their choice.
2. Everyone gathers in a central space.
3. On your signal, challenge everyone to get as close as possible to the person they identified as A (attract). At the same time, they are to stay as far away as possible from the person they identified as R (repel).
4. After 60 to 90 seconds, call time.

Tips for success . . .	➤ Make sure there is plenty of space for the chaos.
	➤ Prompt more movement by asking loudly, "So are you really as far as you can be from your R?" Or "So are you really as close to your A as you can be?"
Try these variations . . .	➤ Play in rounds. In round 1, participants get as close as they can to their A (without regard to their R). In round 2, participants get as far as possible from their R. In round 3, participants get as close to their A and as far from their R as possible.
	➤ See if everyone can somehow be touching their A while staying a certain distance (5 feet?) from their R.
	➤ Use this as an icebreaker activity. Participants' A will be someone they don't know and their R will be someone they know quite well. Participants will introduce themselves to their A.

MAP IT

This is . . .	➤ An activity in which participants form a human map based on where they live.
Use it to . . .	➤ Help groups visualize their proximity to each other outside of work.
Best group size . . .	➤ Unlimited.
Materials you'll need . . .	➤ No materials are necessary for this activity.
Here's how . . .	1. Gather the group in a large, open space. 2. Have participants create a map by standing relative to one another based on where their homes are.
Tips for success . . .	➤ Place something in the middle of the space to represent where they are now. All points will be relative to that point. ➤ Beyond that, don't help or guide anyone; let the group figure it all out. Don't be surprised if someone else steps up and starts to lead, though.
Try these variations . . .	➤ Have participants map where they were born, where they last went on vacation, where they plan to retire, or where their favorite restaurant is. ➤ Have participants map where their work locations are. Afterward, discuss what impact their geographic diversity has on the work they are about to do, if any.

 **OBJECTS**

This is . . . ➤ An activity in which participants in smaller teams find the connection between themselves based on an object they are given.

Use it to . . . ➤ Warm participants up who will be working together later.

Best group size . . . ➤ Unlimited.

Materials you'll need . . . ➤ An object for each team.

Here's how . . .
1. Divide the group into teams of four to seven members.
2. Give each team one object.
3. The teams have 5 minutes to come up with some way that each of them is similar to the object.

For example . . . ➤ "Okay, I think that I'm like that stapler because I can get 'jammed' pretty easily. When you try to staple too fast, it jams and stops working. I'm the same, if you rush me too much, I also 'jam' and basically shut down, unable to work."

Tips for success . . .	➤ The objects can all be the same (each team gets a stapler, for example). Alternatively, each team can work with a different object (one team gets a stapler, one gets a mug, one gets a balloon, etc.).
Try these variations . . .	➤ Rather than relating to the object individually, have the teams make a simile about their object that relates to the topic, the organization, and so forth. For example, "Implementing this project will be like this deck of cards. There will be all sorts of possible combinations of components, which could be confusing. But if we keep our wits about us, we'll be able to sort and organize things brilliantly!"
	➤ After doing this once, have the teams swap items and do it again for another round.
	➤ Rather than supply them with an object, have someone from each team provide the object (something from their pocket or purse?).

OPTIMISTS

This is . . .   ➤ An activity in which participants think of the positive side of a negative comment.

Use it to . . .   ➤ Get the group thinking positively before beginning a potentially negative meeting.

Best group size . . .   ➤ Unlimited.

Materials you'll need . . .   ➤ An index card for each participant.
➤ A pen for each participant.

Here's how . . .
1. Give each participant a card and a pen.
2. Give the group 2 minutes to write down one negative or pessimistic thought about the day, the work, the group, or some other related concept.
3. Have them mingle and pair up immediately.
4. One of the pair reads his or her card to the other.
5. The person read to must then state at least three optimistic, possible outcomes related to the negative thought.
6. The pairs switch roles and repeat steps 4 and 5.

For example . . .
➤ "These meetings always seem to run late!"
➤ "One, this means we'll have to spend less time on the same topics at our next meeting. Two, we'll have less traffic to fight with on our way home,

won't we? Three, well, more time here means less time out on the floor working."

Tips for success . . .	➤ The goal is not to fix any issues, argue about them, or even discuss them. The goal is merely to think of possibilities.
	➤ Give participants an example before they start. The best would be to have someone read his or her card to you, and then you offer three optimistic, possible outcomes.
Try these variations . . .	➤ Have the group break into trios for each round. After the card is read, each person (including the one who read the card) must think of one optimistic possible outcome to share with the others.

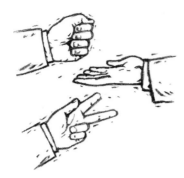

PAPER, SCISSORS, ROCK

This is . . .	➤ An activity in which participants compete with each other to earn tokens.
Use it to . . .	➤ Warm participants up and get them active physically.
Best group size . . .	➤ Unlimited.
Materials you'll need . . .	➤ Five tokens for each participant. ➤ Optional: a small prize.
Here's how . . .	1. Give each participant five tokens. 2. Have everyone pair up. 3. Explain the rules of Paper, Scissors, Rock. 4. Have the pairs play Paper, Scissors, Rock. Whoever wins gets a token from his or her partner. 5. Immediately find another partner and play again. 6. Continue playing until participants either have no more tokens or they have collected 10 tokens.
For example . . .	➤ Players face each other with one fist clenched. They count 1, 2, and 3 together. On each count, they raise and lower their fists slightly (to get into a rhythm). On the third count, they each display

a flat hand (paper), *or* a fist with the index finger and middle finger out straight (scissors), *or* a still-clenched fist (rock). Paper covers (beats) rock. Rock smashes (beats) scissors. Scissors cuts (beats) paper. Ties call for another round(s) until there is a winner.

Tips for success . . .
- The tokens can be pennies, toothpicks, poker chips, straws from the cafeteria, playing cards, a product your organization makes, and so forth.
- Demonstrate a few rounds of Paper, Scissors, Rock with another participant to be sure everyone knows how the game is played.

Try these variations . . .
- Award a prize to the first participant who gets 10 tokens or to the first one who runs out of tokens.
- Don't limit the token accumulation to 10. Play for a certain time, and the winner is whoever has the most tokens. Any ties can be determined by a playoff.
- Eliminate the tokens and prizes. Play the activity just for fun and as a way to force some quick interaction.

THAT'S LIFE

This is . . .   ➤ An activity in which participants take turns responding to two thought-provoking questions.

Use it to . . .   ➤ Get a group warmed up and talking—especially with participants who know each other fairly well already.

Best group size . . .   ➤ Unlimited.

Materials you'll need . . .   ➤ Optional: a pen and piece of paper for each participant.

Here's how . . .
1. Have participants pair up.
2. In pairs, participants take turns finishing the statement "Life is too short to . . ."
3. Participants respond as many times as possible (quick answers are best and often lead to humorous responses).
4. After 60 seconds, have the participants find a new partner and repeat steps 2 and 3.
5. After another 60 seconds, have the participants find yet another new partner and repeat steps 2 through 4. This time, however use the statement, "Life is too short *not* to . . ."

For example . . .	➤ Life is too short to . . . iron sheets; open junk mail; waste it jogging; talk to telemarketers; read the whole newspaper.
	➤ Life is too short *not* to . . . take a cruise somewhere; color with a child; eat as much chocolate as possible; get a massage; watch the sunset.
Tips for success . . .	➤ Give several examples for each statement to get everyone thinking.
	➤ Encourage participants to give quick answers rather than thinking too long and hard. Emphasize quantity over quality.
	➤ It sometimes helps to have the prompting partner repeat the phrase "Life is too short to . . ." before each response is given.
Try these variations . . .	➤ Use different statements: Use "Something I've done that everyone should try is . . ." with "Something I still want to try is . . ." Alternatively, use "One of life's great lessons is . . ." with "One of life's great mysteries is . . ."
	➤ Have participants form teams of three, four, or even five instead of pairs.
	➤ Have participants write their answers down for 2 minutes, and then share with their partner or the rest of the group.

TOPICS

This is . . . ➤ An icebreaker activity in which participants discuss a topic randomly given to them.

Use it to . . . ➤ Help small groups of participants who will work together to warm up to one another.

Best group size . . . ➤ Unlimited.

Materials you'll need . . . ➤ An index card with a topic on it for each team of four to six participants.

Here's how . . .
1. Divide the group into teams of four to six participants.
2. Give one topic card to each team.
3. Allow 5 minutes for teams to share with each other as much as they can about their given topic.

For example . . . ➤ Topics may be the weather, entertainment, sports, food, current events, travel, animals, education, family, competitors of your organization's, health, and so forth.

Tips for success . . . ➤ Create the topic cards in advance. Make more than you think you will need (just in case!).

Try these variations . . .

- ➤ Have the teams swap cards and enjoy another round.
- ➤ Give one blank index card to each team. Have them create a topic card for another team to use.
- ➤ Tell the teams they can't ask their members any questions; they can only make statements about the topic.
- ➤ Have the members in each team take turns making comments. No one can make a second comment until everyone else has made at least one comment about the topic.
- ➤ Prepare several topic cards for each team. After allowing 1–2 minutes for the teams to discuss their first topic, call time. Teams stop, pick the next topic card, and discuss that new topic. Repeat.

INDEX

ABOUT THE AUTHOR

Brian Cole Miller is the founder of Working Solutions in Dublin, Ohio. A sought-after speaker and trainer, he specializes in two areas: developing stronger leaders and building more effective teams. He provides training, coaching, and consulting to busy managers and their teams in companies worldwide, including Anthem Blue Cross Blue Shield, VISA, DuPont, and Nationwide Insurance.

If you have a quick icebreaker or team-building activity that you would like to share with Brian for his next volume, or if you would like to ask questions about this work, please contact Brian Miller at www.WorkingSolutionsOnline.com.

GAYLORD